Semantic Analysis and Understanding of Human Behavior in Video Streaming

Alberto Amato · Vincenzo Di Lecce
Vincenzo Piuri

Semantic Analysis
and Understanding
of Human Behavior
in Video Streaming

Springer

Alberto Amato
Politecnico di Bari
Taranto
Italy

Vincenzo Piuri
Università degli Studi di Milano
Crema
Italy

Vincenzo Di Lecce
Politecnico di Bari
Taranto
Italy

ISBN 978-1-4899-9699-2   ISBN 978-1-4614-5486-1 (eBook)
DOI 10.1007/978-1-4614-5486-1
Springer New York Heidelberg Dordrecht London

Printed on acid-free paper

Springer is part of Springer Science+Business Media (www.springer.com)

Preface

Humans observe, move, and act in the physical world, and interact with objects, other humans, other living beings, and the whole environment to achieve their goals and satisfy their needs and their desires for a fully satisfactory life. A broad spectrum of intertwined mental activities, from fundamental instincts to high-level intellectual reasoning, drives the human choices, actions, and the interactions with the environment, especially in complex situations. Replying to actions only when they have been completed allows for observing their complete effects and have a complete picture of the whole environment, but may create serious problems in the case their outcomes negatively influence the beings and the environment. To prevent these situations a more dynamic interpretation of the outcomes is needed in real time, directly while the actions themselves are still evolving. Interacting with humans implies therefore deducing the goals and the motivations beyond the actions so as to understand their implications and impact and, thus, to decide which reaction is more appropriate.

Understanding the human behavior and the related motivations, goals, and intentions by visually observing movements and actions is a complex cognitive task which involves various aspects of the vision process, the behavior abstraction, and the behavior knowledge-based interpretation. Many neurophysiologists and psychologists have studied the various aspects of the human behavior and its understanding and created conceptual models and descriptions motivating the human actions and interactions.

In the modern society, the information and communication technologies play a key role in supporting our life and our interactions, in augmenting our abilities, and in replicating—at least partially—several of our skills and activities. In this book we focus therefore our attention on the use of these technologies for human motion analysis, recognition, and interpretation, also in real time, as enabling tools for assisting in human behavior understanding and, thus, for building advanced applications based on such understanding. The human motion is typically captured in video streams by observing the scene with appropriate video cameras and other possible supporting devices. Video analytics techniques are used to analyze the video streams to detect and extract events which are related to variations of images in the stream, and not only to the individual images, like the visual cortex does in the human brain on the sequence of images captured by the eyes. Information extracted from the video sequence is then interpreted at a higher abstraction level to achieve the desired understanding of the observed aspects of the human behavior.

Human behavior understanding from video streaming analysis has a huge and continuously growing market. In some cases the impact is so relevant that the expansion of the market is exploding. Currently, this technology is used by a variety of applications, covering a broad spectrum of sectors, e.g., encompassing advanced user interfaces, motion analysis, health care, surveillance, and virtual reality. According to recent studies, video analytics had globally in fact a significant market of US$13.2 billions at the end of 2009 and will reach US$28 by 2013 with a compound annual growth rate of about 22 %. The sector of surveillance systems (including intelligence, surveillance, and reconnaissance) saw government investments worldwide for about US$8 billions in 2011 and is expected to increase of 9 % annually in the USA till 2014. The videogames industry valued US$66 billions worldwide in 2010 and is expected to grow up to US$81 billions by 2016: a significant reason of the current value and the expected grow is due to the motion capture and understanding technologies which are the basis of highly interactive and immersive games and entertainments. These examples show the paramount importance and the humongous and growing economical value of human behavior understanding from the analysis of video streaming, especially for real-time operation. Besides, the increasing availability of capturing devices and high-performance computers at lowering costs make these technologies appealing to a number of new application areas and even open the doors to the invention of new applications, thus increasing even more their market value and impact.

Several applications may greatly benefit from observing human behavior and its understanding through the analysis of video streaming. In the area of advanced user interfaces, understanding human motions and complex actions will allow for creating gesture- and motion-driven interfaces for commanding the operating systems and the applications. This will greatly simplifying the interactions between users and systems since they will become more natural and will not need any specialized device (keyboard, mouse, or similar). This modality will complement and, possibly, integrate the speech interaction, also significantly facilitating people with disabilities. Vision systems may be used in conjunction with speech interactions to solve ambiguous situations. These advanced interfaces greatly simplify and offer more natural the interactions by making computer systems to comprehend the natural human methods of communication, e.g., in entertainment products (especially for advanced interactive games), home automation, social networks, automotive, and transportation.

The understanding of human motion and gestures is also extremely helpful in applications which make extensive use of models and, specifically, which use model-based encoding. For example, in telecommunications video compression for teleconferencing is essential to reduce dramatically the required bandwidth by compacting the image representation and, thus, focusing transmission on the moving parts. Concise representation is helpful also in variable animation control for entertainment and publicity: a few parameters transmitted over the network will allow for describing the whole moving object and controlling its movements. Motion modeling as performance capture is also extremely attractive in games and the entertainment industry to develop products and environments with highly realistic motions both of humans and cartoons by analyzing the motion of real actors. In turn, the reduced required bandwidth will make feasible the use of advanced, interactive applications also in geographical areas, typically the economically less-favored regions, still affected by the digital divide which limits the real-time operations.

Motion analysis is another wide area of application in which capturing and analyzing the human behavior has a significant value and innovation, especially to simplify the observation and to facilitate the development of advanced products. One of the primary market segments will be health care, in which clinical studies of human locomotion, medical diagnosis, medical monitoring (e.g., pre- and post-treatment functional evaluation of patients), and rehabilitation will play a significant role in the market by exploiting the advanced technological support offered by human motion analysis for deepening the understanding of the outcomes of the medical practice. A strictly related segment is assisted living for elders and people with disabilities: motion analysis and understanding will allow for facilitating the interactions and monitoring their activities, thus, for example, detecting possible critical or dangerous situations, medical monitoring, emergencies, and need for help. Another segment related to the medical area is athletes monitoring, with specific focus, e.g., on assisted sport training as well as athletes' motion analysis and optimization: analysis of the sport activities allows for detecting improvements in performance and understanding possible critical aspects of the athlete's movements leading to performance reduction. Motion analysis can be used also in the entertainment industry, e.g., for improving the quality of human motion in choreography of dance and theatre, and for automated indexing of television programs for content-based footage.

Physical security is a very sensitive application area which greatly benefits from human behavior analysis and understanding. In smart surveillance systems, the video streams are analyzed automatically by intelligent approaches which mimic the operation and the skills of surveillance personnel, possibly with constant level of attention and homogeneous (high) level of quality and care, in detecting patterns of unusual behavior and thus deducing the malevolent intentions of people monitored by the video cameras. Indoor and outdoor scenes can be continuously monitored, by assuring safety and protection of persons and goods and, thus, more confidence and trust for a better quality of the daily life. These techniques can be used to protect sensitive locations (e.g., public places, main streets and squares, sports arenas, theatres, cinemas, public meeting places), critical buildings and services (e.g., airports, railways stations, ports, justice and governmental buildings, military buildings, supermarkets, big retail shops, sports halls, universities), and private buildings (e.g., homes). Human behavior analysis for physical security and safety can be exploited also in military, peace-keeping, and humanitarian situations, especially in dangerous areas and during military operations, thus providing support for monitoring the environment and early detection of possible dangers. Intelligence, surveillance, and reconnaissance based on behavior monitoring and understanding are typical application areas for national protection, forensics, and danger and terrorism prevention. In addition to deducing critical or dangerous behavior, human motion observation can be expanded to support person recognition, specifically by using gait recognition, which is sufficiently effective under some environmental and clothing constraints.

Finally, a fruitful market segment, with unique potentials for an even more pervasive and valuable expansion is virtual reality, encompassing a broad variety of specific applications. Motion understanding can be used to create realistic interactive virtual worlds, populated by animated characters which naturally mimic the real counterparts or empower the users to create models very similar to real living beings or behaving in a way very similar to theirs. Animators capture the behavior of human actors and then incorporate their motions in the characters for the virtual environment. Teleconferencing can benefit from a realistic perspective while limiting the bandwidth. Virtual movies and television productions can incorporate characters and special effects based on virtualization and models derived from the analysis of the human behavior and motion. Motion modeling for games and entertainment, especially performance capture, can recreate a realistic environment through virtualized models and interactions; fundamental characteristics may be in fact extracted from the analysis of the human behavior of significant subjects. Virtual and augmented reality (e.g., visual perception test, performing virtual walkthroughs in three-dimensional environments, and training simulations) can be significantly boosted by the extensive use of models and interaction techniques based on information and knowledge provided by human behavior analysis and understanding: in this perspective, robotics, industrial automation, manufacturing, and design can use the virtual environments as a new dimension for interacting with the real world.

This book focus the attention on natural and intuitive human–computer interaction and, more specifically, to the problem of real-time, vision-based behavior analysis and human motion recognition and interpretation. This will constitute the underlying methodology to capture knowledge from the external environment and exploit information and models within advanced applications, like those mentioned above.

Simplifying the behavior analysis by means of a symbolic representation will make viable the scene monitoring and the human behavior understanding in online operations. The research methodology developed in this book is in fact based on the hierarchical decomposition of the human behavior. Scene analysis and behavior understanding are performed by using a symbolic interpretation of the visual input: images from the captured video streams are described by means of strings of symbols and the grammar-based analysis methodology allows for hierarchical decomposition and parsing of the visual input. The proposed framework is flexible enough to provide analysis at various abstraction levels of the observed scenes (encompassing the scene level, the level of the group of objects, and the level of the individual object), thus offering a structured approach suited for various points of view at different granularity.

Contents

Chapter 1
Introduction

This book proposes a new methodology to automatically analyze human behavior in narrow domains using video streaming. This chapter begins discussing the main technological innovations that arc creating the premise to implement such kind of systems. Next, the principal application fields of these systems are briefly presented and then the main issues that the scientific community are facing to realize them are presented. Finally the proposed methodology is briefly presented and the remaining part of the book is outlined.

1.1 Introduction

Aim of this book is to investigate, both from a theoretical and a technological point of view, the problem of human behavior analysis in video streaming. From a psychological point of view, the general concept of "behavior" is the reaction of human beings to a set of external and internal impulses. These impulses may be caused by very different sources, and only the combination of them can represent an objective explanation of the observed behavior.

In the latest years, information and communication technology (ICT) has had a strong improvement having significant influence on our everyday life. The effects of the technological improvements in the fields of sensor manufacturing and communication networks are particularly relevant. For what concerns the latter, nowadays is the "Internet Age". Millions of computers are connected among them, sharing data and hosting services for a large number of users living everywhere in the world. Furthermore, the network is becoming pervasive. Indeed, thanks to the spread of wireless networks it is possible to be "connected" everywhere also by means of devices which are different from the traditional PC (notebook, netbook, smartphone, etc.).

A. Amato et al., *Semantic Analysis and Understanding of Human Behavior in Video Streaming*, DOI: 10.1007/978-1-4614-5486-1_1,
© Springer Science+Business Media New York 2013

For what concerns sensors, in these days there is a fast evolution toward smaller sensors and with increasing performance, e.g., in terms of precision, accuracy, and reliability. This has led to the development of a large number of applications. For example, nowadays the major part of videos and pictures are taken by using digital devices, while sensors and actuators based on the Micro Electro-Mechanical Systems (MEMS) technology are the key elements of many applications for the modern smartphones.

These factors have also enabled and booted the development of sensor networks that are able to monitor wide areas where human beings perform their activities. Studying data recorded by these sensor networks we can develop technologies and systems for high semantic level analysis of the human behavior [1]. The aim of these technologies consists of defining a description of the human behavior that can be used in recognition tasks. Human behavior analysis can be coupled with biometric systems [2–7] in order to recognize also the identity of the person performing a given action. On the other hand it should be noticed that this kind of system could have a strong influence on the privacy. For the interested reader, an in depth analysis of this aspect can be found in [8–12].

The analysis from a psychological point of view of the reasons that have determined a given behavior is beyond the scope of these technologies.

In the latest years, automatic human behavior analysis has attracted the interest of the international scientific community. This strong interest is due to the many potential applications that such kind of systems can have. Essentially, these applications can be divided into three macro areas:

- *Surveillance*. This application area has a relevant interest also due to the facts characterizing the history of the last decade. In particular, the aim of the applications in this area is monitoring and understanding human behavior in public and crowded areas (such as streets, bus and train stations, airports, shopping malls, sport arenas, and museums). These applications can be used both for management (for example: evaluation of crowding in the monitored areas, human flow analysis, and detection of the congestion points) and security (for example: human behavior analysis, activity recognition of individuals and groups, and detection of suspicious persons) [13].
- *Control*. In this area the researchers try to develop systems that are able to evaluate some human motion parameters (i.e. speed, gait) and/or the poses (i.e. the mutual position of the harms, or the position of the head) to control actions and/or operations [14]. One of the most important fields of application for these systems is the human–machine interaction. On the market there are some interesting uses as input devices for videogames. These devices use both video and inertial sensors to evaluate the player's motion and understand his/her commands.
- *Analysis*. Applications of human motion analysis are used in various fields, including: sports (as an aid for evaluating the techniques and the performance of the athletes), and medicine (as an aid in the diagnosis of problems in human postures and in the orthopedic rehabilitation) [15].

The economic and social relevance of potential applications (especially the security, entertainment, and medical ones), the scientific complexity, the speed and price of current hardware intensified the effort within the scientific community towards automatic capture and analysis of human motion.

In the literature, various approaches have been proposed to capture the human behavior. Most of them use video sensors since these technologies are not invasive and rather cheap, as well as they produce good-quality data suited for being processed by means of inference techniques mimicking the human ones. Some authors proposed alternative approaches by using other kind of sensors, such as inertial sensors, audio sensors, presence detectors; unfortunately, these sensors (often installed in devices as "wearable sensors") are characterized by some invasiveness and, therefore, can be used only in some specific control applications [16, 17]. Consequently, for these reasons, this book addresses the human behavior analysis by using video streaming as the most appropriate technology to observe the human behavior.

Automatic understanding of the human behavior from video sequences is a very challenging problem since it implies understanding, identifying, and either mimicking the neuro-physiological and psychological processes, which are naturally performed in humans or creating similar outcomes by means of appropriate information and knowledge processing. In order to achieve this goal the problem has been split into two steps:

1. A compact representation of the real world is first defined by using the data sampled by cameras. This representation should be as close as possible to the reality, view invariant, and reliable for subsequent processing. A video streaming contains a large amount of data, but often they are redundant and/or useless for the human behavior analysis (for example: the static data about the background scene is not helpful). Therefore, it is necessary to track the areas where a difference between two successive video frames has been detected in order to focus the attention on the areas in which there are moving objects (may be humans), while discarding the background with irrelevant information. Later these moving entities will be identified as human beings or unanimated objects (or animals). Moving entities will be traced through the various frames to characterize their movements.

2. By starting from the representation defined in the first step, the visual information will be interpreted for recognizing and learning the human behavior. Various techniques have been proposed in the literature to define appropriate behavior reference models. In these approaches, recognition will consist in comparing an unknown input to the models by using suitable distance functions. The nearest model to the input is considered as the class to which the observed behavior belongs. The main limits of this approach are:

   - there is a finite number of recognizable behaviors (as many as the number of the models defined before using the system);
   - a large number of training sequences are usually required in order to define a model in a sufficiently accurate and recognizable way;

- it is not possible to automatically associate a meaning to an observed behavior;
- it is not possible to generalize the learnt models and infer new behaviors from the learnt ones.

Therefore, the efforts of the scientific community are focused on studying systems in which the knowledge of the considered behavior reference models is built incrementally, i.e., by starting from an empty set of models, new behavior models are, first, identified by observing people's activities and considering the current behavior knowledge and, then, added to the current behavior knowledge. When models have been learnt, the system will be able to recognize them and similar behaviors in the future.

Nowadays, both of the above steps are open research fields. At this time, there is not a comprehensive and universally valid method to obtain the representation of the real-world behaviors. Even the most suitable type of sensors to be used is still under discussion. This is basically due to the lack of a general solution to two important problems: the sensory gap and the semantic gap.

The sensory gap is the difference between the real world and its representation obtained by using data sampled by sensors [18]. For example, by using a camera, a bi-dimensional representation of the real world can be obtained, while our eyes give us a three-dimensional model. To address this problem researchers are proposing various data fusion techniques based, for example, on two or more cameras, or on hybrid vision systems (cameras plus other kinds of sensor).

The semantic gap is the difference between the behavior description used by human beings and the computational model used by the human behavior analysis systems [19]. To solve this problem or at least to reduce the effects of this gap, researchers have been working on exploiting some knowledge about scene and/or the human behavior, thus narrowing the huge variety of possible behavioral patterns by focusing on a specific narrow domain.

This book addresses therefore the analysis and understanding of the human behavior by considering the various aspects, issues and implications depicted above, both from the theoretical perspective and from the point of view of technological supports. The aim is to provide solid foundations for implementing efficient and effective human behavior analysis and understanding systems, suitable for a variety of applications encompassing, e.g., video surveillance, medical applications, human–machine interface, and entertainment.

In the above perspectives, this book gives two highly-significant, innovative, and original contributions to the human behavior analysis and understanding in video streaming:

1. A new method to perform images fusion in multi-camera systems, by identifying the corresponding points in the various images without the assumption of epipolar geometry. This assumption is fundamental for many works on this topic but it imposes strong constraints on the camera positions (an in depth presentation of this problem is proposed in the Chap. 4). The proposed method does not introduce this constraint. This fact makes this method applicable to

many existing multi-camera acquisition systems. Using this method it is possible to mitigate some aspects of the sensory gap, like the target partial occlusions in crowding scenes. From this point of view, it can be seen as a method to improve the performance of the semantic analysis because it allows for enhancing the performance of the tracking algorithm (a step in the processing chain for human behavior analysis). By the other hands, it should be stressed the fact that the kernel of the book is the semantic analysis of the human behavior in video streaming and that the proposed approach can work also without this module and so, also using a single camera system.

2. A new approach to analysis and understanding by using the syntactical symbolic analysis of images and video streaming described by means of strings of symbols. This allows for high simplicity in the scene and motion descriptions so that the behavior analysis will have limited computational complexity, thanks to the intrinsic nature both of the representations and the related operations used to manipulate them. On the other hand, this approach has a great flexibility. Indeed, it allows for performing a hierarchical analysis of the recorded scenes defining a different grammar for each level. At the higher level, the behavior of the human beings moving in the scene is analyzed studying their motion parameters (the trajectory that they are following). In this way it is possible to have an analysis of scenario considering the moving objects and their interactions. At the lowest level, the system can produce a detailed analysis of the action taken by each single human being in the scene. According to the complexity of the task, between these two levels, it is possible to define as many intermediate levels as they are necessary. This hierarchical analysis can exploit the full potentiality of the modern video surveillance systems where there is a fixed camera of scenario and one or more moving cameras that can focus their attention on some areas of interest. In this application, the first level of the proposed hierarchy is applied to the camera of scenario and the second to the moving cameras.

To show the effectiveness of the proposed approach and technology, a demonstrative system has been implemented and applied to some real indoor environments with significant results.

The proposed approach is not tailored on a single specific operating environment, but has a high flexibility and is able to deal with a large number of applications, thus being of unique value as a new fundamental enabling technology. This has been possible since the proposed approach works at a high abstraction level on the semantic analysis of the human behaviors, also exploiting the advantages offered by the image fusion in multi-camera systems (which are becoming increasingly popular due to their decreasing costs). For example, in surveillance the proposed approach enables the creating of innovative systems which are able to evaluate the danger level of observed situations from a semantic point of view, thus significantly enhancing the correctness and completeness of alarms. In control applications it supports the implementation of adaptive, advanced human–machine interfaces since the motion of human beings can be analyzed in a fully automatic way. In analysis applications, the proposed approach can be used as an advanced enabling technology for implementing systems, e.g., for sport actions evaluation and automatic video indexing.

This book reports the accomplished research and, in particular, the theoretical foundations, the technology, the innovative approach, the experiments, and the achieved results. This book is structured as follows.

- Chapter 2 presents a brief overview of the sensors which can be used for human behavior analysis.
- Chapter 3 reviews the current state of the art in sensor data processing, image fusion, and human behavior analysis and understanding.
- Chapter 4 describes the proposed method for using multi-camera system in semantic analysis applications.
- Chapter 5 presents the method used for semantic analysis of human behavior.
- The experimental evaluation and the obtained results are presented in Chap. 6.
- Conclusions and future works are reported in Chap. 7.

Chapter 2
Sensors for Human Behavior Analysis

This chapter proposes a brief description of the most common sensors used in literature to perform the automatic analysis of the human behavior. For each kind of sensor, at least a scientific work using it for human behavior analysis is presented. This chapter helps the readers to understand because the author has focused his attention on the analysis of human behavior using video streaming.

2.1 Motivation

Automatic human behavior analysis and recognition are complex tasks that have attracted a lot of researchers in the latest years. One of the primary tasks to perform implementing such analysis is to define a representation of the real world using the data sampled by some sensors.

Nowadays the most frequently used sensors are camera devices, but in literature there are also approaches based on the employment of other kinds of sensor. These approaches achieve good results in some specific domains but often they cannot be generalized to other contexts. In literature, there are many works applying data fusion techniques to build complex systems based on using different type of sensors [20–22].

In this chapter a brief overview about the following sensors and of the works using them is presented: Radio Frequencies Identifier (RFID), pressure sensors, Micro-Electro-Mechanical Systems (MEMS) and image sensors.

The aim of this brief overview is to show the most important used sensors in human behavior analysis, their applications and their limits. This discussion should help the readers to understand because the author has focused his attention on the analysis of human behavior using video streaming. The main goal of the book is the semantic analysis of video streaming. From this point of view, since the sensors play a secondary role in this book, a critical overview of the literature about sensors is beyond the scope of this book.

A. Amato et al., *Semantic Analysis and Understanding of Human Behavior in Video Streaming*, DOI: 10.1007/978-1-4614-5486-1_2, © Springer Science+Business Media New York 2013

2.2 Radio Frequencies Identifier Technology

RFID is the acronym of Radio Frequencies Identifier. This technology is based on four key elements: the RFID tags themselves, the RFID readers, the antennas and choice of radio characteristics, and the computer network (if any) that is used to connect the readers.

RFID tags are devices composed of an antenna and a small silicon chip containing a radio receiver, a radio modulator for sending a response back to the reader, control logic, some amount of memory, and a power system. A RFID tag transmits the data stored inside its memory module when it is exposed to radio waves of the correct frequency sent by the reader.

According to the used power system there are two kinds of tags: passive tags where the power system can be completely powered by the incoming RF signal and active tags where the tag's power system has a battery. Passive tags are cheaper than active tags but they have a shorter range of action (the reader must be positioned very close to the tag).

Figure 2.1 shows a diagram of the power system for a passive inductively coupled transponder-RFID tag. An inductively coupled transponder comprises an electronic data-carrying device, usually a single microchip, and a large area coil that functions as an antenna. The reader's antenna coil generates a strong, high frequency electromagnetic field, which penetrates the cross-section of the coil area and the area around the coil. The antenna coil of the transponder and the capacitor C_1 form a resonant circuit tuned to the transmission frequency of the reader. The voltage U at the transponder coil reaches a maximum due to resonance step-up in the parallel resonant circuit. The layout of the two coils can also be interpreted as a transformer (transformer coupling), in which case there is only a very weak coupling between the two windings.

The simplest RFID chips contain only a serial number. This serial number is written into the chip by the manufacturer but there are also tags where this code can be written by the end user. An example of this code is the EPC (Electronic Product Code) that is a number composed of 96 bits. This number is the kernel of an international standard making RFID technology a pillar element of the inter-national logistic chain. This standard is under the oversight of EPCglobal Inc[TM] a not-for-profit joint venture between GS1 (formerly EAN International) and GS1 US (formerly the Uniform Code Council).

More sophisticated RFID chips can contain read-write memory that can be programmed by a reader

Among the various applications where RFID technology is used, there is also the human activity detection and monitoring, an example of such applications is [23]. In this work the authors propose a system to detect the activity of daily living performed at home. This is a challenging task for various reasons such as: each one can perform the same action in different ways, there are many possible activities that a system should model with minimum human effort, etc. The key observation done by the authors is that the sequence of objects that a person uses performing a

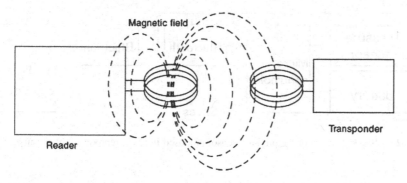

Fig. 2.1 A block diagram of a RFID tag

given activity is a good marker both of the action type and quality. Starting from this observation they propose a system composed of three modules: specialized sensors to detect object interactions, a probabilistic engine that infers activities given observations from sensors, and a model creator to create probabilistic models of activities. In this work the used sensors are RFID tags attached on each object of interest. The RFID reader is built inside a glove that the user should wear while performing his activities of daily living. The system was tested on 14 predefined activities and the obtained results showed good performance both in terms of precision (88 %) and recall (73 %).

Despite these good results the system presents various limits. From a techno-logical point of view, water and metal absorb the radio waves that most RFID tags use; metal can also short-circuit the tag antenna. This fact limits the number of correctly observable actions. But the most important limitation of this approach is that it is too invasive. Indeed it requires that the user must wear a glove. This can be a serious problem due to the fact that many people are not too attracted by using gloves while performing activities of daily living.

2.3 Pressure Sensors

Pressure transducers are very common and cheap. They are used in various applications and they work using various principles (variation of capacity, varia-tion of resistance, piezoelectric, etc.).

In [24] the authors propose a human behavior recognition system using a set of pressure sensors based on the variation of resistance. For this kind of sensors the conversion of pressure into an electrical signal is achieved by the physical deformation of strain gages which are bonded into the diaphragm of the pressure transducer and wired into a Wheatstone bridge configuration. Pressure applied to the pressure transducer produces a deflection of the diaphragm which introduces strain to the gages. The strain will produce an electrical resistance change proportional to the pressure.

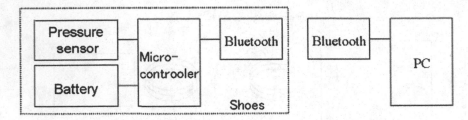

Fig. 2.2 A block diagram of the pressure sensor proposed in [24]. (reproduced by permission of IEEE)

Figure 2.2 shows a block diagram of the whole pressure measurement system proposed in [24]. The transducer is connected to a microcontroller that is able to communicate with a standard PC using a Bluetooth link. A serious constrain for this system is its power supply module that is composed of a 9 V alkaline battery. This fact introduces the well known limitations due to the lifecycle of the battery, maintenance, etc.

The main idea at the base of this work is that measuring the plantar pressure distribution it is possible to infer information about the actions performed by the user. Four sensors were installed in each shoe. According to the authors, it is possible to classify fifteen different behaviors: walking (slow, normal, fast), running (slow, normal, fast) standing (leaning forward, load on tiptoe, upright), leaning standing to one foot (leaning forward, normal), sitting (bending forward, normal), floating, and no wearing. The parameters used to classify the various actions are pressure values and length of time where a given pressure is measured. These parameters are compared to a fixed set of thresholds to identify the various actions.

According to the authors, the system achieves good classification rate (about 90 % of successfully classifications) but the experiment settings are not well described. The main limits of this approach are the necessity of a calibration stage for each person to define the various thresholds and its invasivity (indeed the measuring system is installed in the shoes and it is quite visible). These considerations make the system not suitable for applications in everyday life situations.

2.4 Micro Electro-Mechanical Systems Sensors

Micro-Electro-Mechanical Systems (MEMS) are devices built by means of the integration of mechanical elements, sensors, actuators, and electronics on a common silicon substrate through micro-fabrication technology. The current leaders in commercially successful MEMS technology are accelerometers. These devices are used in a large number of applications such as: automotive industry, inertial navigation systems, cellular phones, etc.

The physical mechanisms underlying MEMS accelerometers include capacitive, electromagnetic, piezoelectric, ferroelectric, optical, etc. The most successful types are based on capacitive transduction; the reasons are the simplicity of the sensor element itself, no requirement for exotic materials, low power consumption, and good stability over temperature.

These sensors are used in many applications involving the so-called "wearable-sensors". For example, in [25] the authors propose a system to classify the human pose in "sitting", "standing" and "walking" using a bi-axial accelerometer attached to the user's thigh. The sensor is positioned in order to measure the gravity acceleration using the Y-axis when the user is in "standing" position and the X-axis when she/he is in "sitting" position. The "walking" action is detected when the variance of acceleration is greater than a predefined threshold.

Reference [26] presents a method to detect physical activities from data acquired using five small biaxial accelerometers worn simultaneously on different parts of the body. In particular the sensors are placed on each subject's right hip, dominant wrist, non-dominant upper arm, dominant ankle, and non-dominant thigh to recognize ambulation, posture, and other everyday activities.

The experiments carried-out aim at identifying twenty different actions of everyday life (see [26] for further details). The system was tested on twenty subjects from the academic community volunteered. Data was collected from 13 males and 7 females. Data were classified using various methods but decision tree classifiers showed the best performance recognizing everyday activities with an overall accuracy rate of 84 %. Interestingly, the obtained results show that some activities are recognized well with subject-independent training data while others appear to require subject-specific training data.

2.5 Image Sensors

This kind of sensors are used in all the cameras and camcorders used to create still images and video streaming. The kernel of this kind of sensors consists of an array of tiny pixels (Picture Elements). Sensor pixels are composed of photodiodes.

During the imaging process, the light starts to fall on photodiodes, and they convert photons into electric charge. Photodiodes are not sensible to color, so digital cameras use different color filters to transmit light through. The most common ones are filters for three basic colors: red, green and blue. So, the camera is able to calculate the number of photons of three basic colors that fell on each photodiode while the camera shutter was open. To calculate all color components around each photodiode, red, green and blue filters should be situated adjacently. This makes it possible to convert raw image data into a full-color image in RGB (Red Green Blue) space.

The most common type of color filter array is called a "Bayer array". This filter gives priority to the green mimicking the behavior of human eyes. A schematic overview of the imaging process is shown in Fig. 2.3. The light is filtered by an infra red filter (Fig. 2.3). The filtered light goes through a Bayer array filter and finally hits the pixels of the sensor.

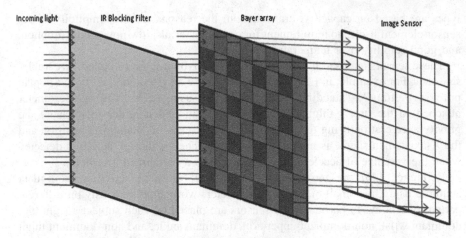

Fig. 2.3 A schematic view of an image sensor. **a**—IR-Blocking Filter, **b**—Color Filters, **c**—Color blind sensors, **d**—The image sensor composed of millions of light sensors

Nowadays, the image sensors are built using two technologies: CCD (Charge-Coupled Device) and CMOS (Complementary Metal–Oxide–Semiconductor). Both the technologies use photodiodes to convert light in electrons, but they use two different methods to read these values from each pixel of the sensor. In a CCD device, the charge is actually transported across the chip and read at one corner of the array. A special manufacturing process is used to create the ability of transporting charges across the chip without distortion. This process leads to very high-quality sensors in terms of fidelity and light sensitivity. In most CMOS devices, there are several transistors at each pixel that amplify and move the charge using more traditional wires. The CMOS approach is more flexible because each pixel can be read individually. CCD sensors give better images than CMOS sensors but the latter are cheaper than the former. Furthermore, in the last years the quality difference between the images sampled by these family of sensors are becoming smaller indeed, ever more often CMOS sensors are used in good quality cameras.

Most of the works in literature on human behavior analyze video streaming sampled using these image sensors. The next chapter proposes a review of such works.

2.6 Summary

This chapter has presented a brief and not exhaustive overview of the sensors used in some applications of human behavior analysis. Some sensors have been omitted because they are often used in conjunction with video analysis by means of data fusion techniques. Two relevant examples of such sensors are: audio and multi-spectral sensors.

Audio sensors are becoming ever more interesting due to progress in speech recognition. In literature it is possible to find their applications for the recognition of specific human behaviors. For example, in [27] a system to detect aggressions in trains is proposed while in [28] a method for action detection in action movies is described. Furthermore, audio-vision data are used to detect human emotions as shown in [29] where the system is able to detect 4 cognitive states (interest, boredom, frustration and puzzlement) and 7 prototypical emotions (neural, happiness, sadness, anger, disgust, fear and surprise).

Multi-spectral sensors are used in many remote sensing applications. In human behavior analysis there is a strong interest to infrared sensors because they can operate in total darkness allowing for the person detection during the night. In [30] a data fusion approach working on infrared images and classical CCD camera images is presented.

The sensors presented in this chapter are used in systems called wearable sensors. These kind of systems are intrusive (because the user are required to wear the sensors) and so they can be applied only in some restricted applications (such as human–machine interface applications).

Multi-spectral sensors can give excellent results but they are too expensive to be used in real world applications.

Audio sensors are cheap but they are not able to give good results in terms of human activity detection without using some data fusion techniques with video streaming. But these systems have a high computational cost due to the complexity of the used algorithm.

For these reasons, in this book, only approaches based on video streaming analysis will be considered.

Chapter 3
Related Work

This chapter proposes an overview of the literature about the automatic human behavior analysis using streaming video. The discussion starts presenting the processing chain used to implement such kind of systems and then the attention is focused only on the works aiming at semantic analysis. The works presented in this chapter are classified in: scene interpretation, human recognition and action primitives and grammars. For each class a brief introductive description is provided and some relevant works are analyzed to give an idea of the proposed approaches and of the difficulties that they face. Finally, the chapter ends with a discussion about the state of the art in this field and with a brief overview of the specific challenges that this book is addressing.

3.1 Introduction

Even though in literature there are many works on human behavior analysis and recognition, this is still an open research field. This is due to the inherent complexity of such task. Indeed, human behavior recognition can be seen as the vertex of a computational pyramid as shown in Fig. 3.1. Each level of this pyramid takes in input the output of the lower one and gives an output that can be used as input for the upper level or as a standalone application. The lowest level takes in input the raw video streams and gives in output a map of the image region where a moving object is detected. Climbing up this pyramid, the semantic level of performed tasks grows up. The processes at the lowest level work with **moving region** in a single frame while those at the second level work identifying **objects** in the same frame. At the third level a new parameter plays an important role: the **time**. Indeed, the processes at this level work associating the detected moving objects in the current frame with those in the previous one, providing temporal trajectories through the state space. The output of this level is sent to the human behavior analysis module.

A. Amato et al., *Semantic Analysis and Understanding of Human Behavior in Video Streaming*, DOI: 10.1007/978-1-4614-5486-1_3,
© Springer Science+Business Media New York 2013

Fig. 3.1 A hierarchical
overview of the
computational chain for
human behavior recognition

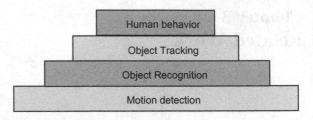

Fig. 3.1 A hierarchical
overview of the
computational chain for
human behavior recognition

Each level of this processing pyramid has its own characteristics and difficulties often due the partial completeness of the used data (for example: the tentative to extract 3D data about moving objects working on 2D images).

In the following paragraphs, a brief overview of the main issues related to each level is presented.

3.2 Motion Detection

These algorithms find the moving areas computing the difference at pixel level between the current frame and a background model. This model can be a fixed frame (useful for indoor applications) or a complex model where each pixel is defined by a Gaussian probability distribution [31].

A good background model should be enough robust to handle rapid illumination changes in the scene and at the same time should be able to recognize permanent changes (for example a chair that was moved from its previous position) as quick as possible.

The frame differencing between adjacent frames in a video streaming is a well studied approach. Starting from a sequence of frames of a given video streaming $I = \{I_1, I_2, ..., I_n\}$, where I_j is a the jth frame, an algorithm for motion detection gives as output a binary map (often called change mask) identifying changed regions in the last image according to the following generic rule:

$$M(x) = \begin{cases} 1 & \textit{if there is a significant change at pixel } x \textit{ of } I_j \\ 0 & \textit{otherwise} \end{cases}$$

In literature this problem has been studied for a long time, indeed, since the late 70s it is possible to find an interesting work [32] based on the frame differencing of temporally adjacent frames. This kind of approach shows serious limits when applied in scenes where the condition of luminosity is not constant. This fact limit's the field of application of such technique.

A strong performance improvement has been achieved in the 1997 with the work [33]. In this work the authors propose a system working in indoor environment. They propose to model the area surrounding the moving object (namely the background) as a texture surface, so, each point on the texture surface is associated with a mean color value and a distribution about that mean. The color distribution of each pixel is modeled with the Gaussian described by a full covariance matrix. This background model is continuously updated using a simple adaptive filter. In this way it is possible to compensate for changes in lighting, and even for object movement (for example a book moved from a position to another).

The main drawback of this approach is the fact that it is not suitable for modeling outdoor scenes because they are characterized by a strong variability due to lighting changes, repetitive motions from clutter, and long-term scene changes.

A substantial improvement in background modeling is achieved by using multimodal statistical models to describe per-pixel background color. For instance, in [34], the authors use a mixture of Gaussians to model the pixel color. In this work, the value of each pixel is modeled as a mixture of Gaussian. Analyzing the persistence and the variance of each of the Gaussians of the mixture, it is possible to state which Gaussian may correspond to the background colors. The set of the pixels with values that do not fit the background distributions are considered as foreground until there is not a Gaussian that includes them with sufficient, consistent evidence supporting it to convert it to a new background mixture.

In order to improve the robustness to camera jitter and small movements in the background, in [35] the pixel background is modeled using a non parametric kernel density estimation. In this work, during the process of background subtraction, each pixel is matched both with the corresponding pixel in the background and with the neighborhood pixels. There are also approaches using other features. For example, in [36] the authors propose to use also the texture analysis in the background subtraction process. This approach is motivated by the fact that typically the texture is a feature quite robust against the changing in light conditions.

3.3 Object Detection and Representation

Object detection: These algorithms identify moving objects analyzing the moving areas detected by the previous module. Typically, they classify the pixels in the moving areas in: shadows, moving object, cast shadow from moving object, ghost object (false positive), and ghost shadow. Some examples of criterions used to classify the pixels are color and gradients [37] and motion flow analysis [38].

An object detection algorithm should be characterized by high precision in the classification of each pixel of the scene. In order to achieve this goal a background model should be able to detect the shape with great accuracy and it should be as fast as possible in reacting to changes in time. The latter ability is useful to avoid that a sudden position change of an object in the scene is erroneously considered a moving object (transient background case) while the former one helps in the successive steps of object identification and tracking.

The following figures shows the results of an experiment carried out in an indoor environment aiming at clarify some aspects of object detection algorithms.

For the sake of simplicity, let us consider as background model a fixed frame of a video sequence where there are not moving objects (see Fig. 3.2).

Fig. 3.2 The frame used as background model

In this experiment a background subtraction algorithm has been used to identify the moving objects and no a priori knowledge is used to identify the objects.

Figure 3.3 shows a generic frame *I* with a moving object (a walking man) and Fig. 3.4 shows the output of the object detection algorithm applied to that frame. This algorithm can be improved to obtain a better shape of the moving object but this exceeds the scope of this book. Analyzing Fig. 3.4 it is possible to say that the algorithm has successfully individuate the moving object in the frame *I*, so, while a man is walking in this room, the object detection algorithm is able to identify it.

The figures sequence starting from Figs. 3.5, 3.6, 3.7, 3.8 shows an example of the genesis of the ghost into the output of this kind of algorithms. In Fig. 3.5, the walking man starts to interact with a fixed object in the scene: a chair. In this simple background model, the chair was considered as part of the background.

In Fig. 3.7 the man ends its action. He has moved the chair from a position to another one. Analyzing the output of the object detection algorithm in Fig. 3.8, the presence of a ghost is observable, indeed both the old and the new position of the chair are considered as "moving areas". The old area is the ghost object.

Figure 3.8 requires some observations. In which extent is it correct to consider the chair a fixed object or a moving one? A possible answer to this question can be the following one: the chair should be considered a fixed object until the man does not move it. Then it should be considered a moving object while the man is moving it and finally, it should be considered a fixed object again when the man leaves it).

Fig. 3.3 An example of moving object in a frame (*a walking man*)

This fact requires the implementation of adaptive background models that are able to distinguish between "real" moving objects and background objects that are moved from a place to another. An example of such a system can be found in [38] where the motion flow analysis is used to detect the ghosts (indeed, referring to the example shown Fig. 3.8, it is clear that the speed of the chair ghost is equal to zero).

3.4 Object Tracking

Aim of the algorithms for object tracking is to compute the trajectory of each moving object in a scene by identifying their positions in each frame of the video sequence. Difficulties in tracking objects can arise due to abrupt object motion, changing appearance patterns of the object and/or the scene, object-to-object and object-to-scene occlusions, etc.

The two key elements of the methods for object tracking are: the chosen approach for object representation and the algorithm used for tracking the objects after the appropriate representation has been defined.

The most widely used models for object representation are:

Fig. 3.4 The result of the object detection algorithm applied to the frame shown in Fig. 3.3

- **points**: the entire object is represented by some relevant points. The barycenter is
  used when the moving object represents a small area inside the whole frame and/
  or when this representation is suitable for the scope of the highest level tasks of the
  computational process (see Fig. 3.1). Another interesting approach is based on
  using a set of points to represent each shape and/or image. These points are often
  called "interest points". An interest point is a point inside a shape and/or image
  that has a well defined position and can be robustly detected. Typical examples of
  interest points are: corners, isolated points characterized by local minima or
  maximum of luminosity, line endings or points on a curve where the curvature has
  a ridge, or a maximal, etc. The interest points are often used to characterize the
  entire image for example in image retrieval applications [39, 40], but they are also
  used in object tracking to model the various shapes [41]. An efficient interest
  points detector algorithm must be robust respect to changes in the shape, size and
  orientation of the various objects where the interest points lie on. In literature a
  large number of interest points detectors have been proposed [42–45]. In particular, in [45] the authors propose a novel method showing good robustness to shape
  rotation, scaling and noise. This method is based on the analysis of the local
  frequency representation of an image. Local frequency is the spatial derivative of
  the local phase, where the local phase of any signal can be found from its Hilbert
  transform. In order to identify the interest points, a threshold is then applied to the
  local frequency map, obtained analyzing the neighborhood of each pixel using an
  adaptive mask.

Fig. 3.5 The moving object starts an action on a fixed object (*a chair*)

The results shown in Fig. 3.9 demonstrate the robustness of this approach to rotation, scale and noise. In particular, Fig. 3.9a shows the original image (a gray scale image often used as test-bed for this kind of algorithms), Figure 3.9b presents the local frequency image obtained applying the proposed method to the original image, and finally Fig. 3.9c shows the detected interest points. Figure 3.9d, e demonstrate the robustness of the method to the rotation indeed they show the results obtained applying the same algorithm to the image rotated by 45° and 115°. Figure 3.9f, g present the results obtained after a scale operation (respectively a scale factor of 1.2 and 2 has been used). The robustness to noise is shown in Fig. 3.9h, i where a Signal to Noise Ratio (SNR) of 19 and 40 dB are respectively applied to the input image. It is possible to notice that the detected interest points are almost the same in all the conditions.

- **Primitive geometric shapes**: the object is represented by a bounding elementary shape such as rectangle or ellipse. This kind of approach is often used to model the motion of rigid objects (i.e., car in traffic monitoring applications). In literature there are many works on this topic such as [46–48]. One of the most widely used approach used by algorithms falling in this category is the kernel based object tracking. The key features of this approach are: low computation cost, easy implementation and competitive performance. One of the main drawbacks of these algorithms is that they are not robust to changes in scale representation. There are some works that tried to face this problem but, as well explained in

Fig. 3.6 The result of the object detection algorithm applied to the frame shown in Fig. 3.5

[49] often they obtain poor results. In particular, some used approaches fail in finding the right operating scale and they makes object scale shrink too small or grow too large. In [46] the authors propose a method to overcome this problem. Starting from the scale space theory proposed in [50], they used scale space as the corresponding space to construct the mean shift based iterative procedure. This choice has been done because, scale space theory provides a robust and effective way to select the best scales for discriminating features in image plane. Furthermore, from a computational point of view, using the Gaussian kernel, there are a many efficient methods to generate scale space (i.e., a pre-computed look-up table) and, from the point of view of the stability, the Gaussian function outperform many other function such as the sigmoid function. Figure 3.10 is extracted from. In this figure, a comparative evaluation between the results obtained in [51] (Fig. 3.10.) and those obtained in (Fig. 3.10b) are shown. This figure shows how the method based on the scale space theory (Fig. 3.10b) outperform the first one (Fig. 3.10a) in handling image scaling.

- **object silhouette and contour**: the object is represented by its contour and/or by its silhouette (namely the area inside the object contour). Various contour tracking approaches have been proposed in computer vision literature. One of the widely used methods was introduced in [52]. This work introduces the so called snake model. The snake is a spline that is defined minimizing a given energy function. This function considers three main contributes: the internal

Fig. 3.7 The moving object ends the action started in Fig. 3.5 (*it moved a chair*)

energy of the spline that introduces a piecewise smoothness constraint; the image force that are used to push the snake near various relevant image features such as lines, edges, etc.; external constraint forces used to position the snake near local minimum. This work has obtained good results and can be considered the starting point of many other approaches trying to modify the energy function such as [53, 54] and, at some extent also to other works proposing variations on the function to minimize [55]. The main limit of this kind of approaches is that the energy function handling the contour evolution can fall in local minima and so they are sensitive at the starting conditions.

Another possible approach consists in using some parametric models of the contour. As it is shown in [56], these methods can obtain good performance when the topology of the extracted contour is simple.

In literature there are also other approaches identifying directly the object silhouette rather than its contour [57, 58]. In particular in [57] the authors propose a method working without a priori knowledge about the target objects and both the target and the background can vary its appearance. Furthermore, the method is robust also to camera movement. The method works estimating the target silhouette every frame trying to minimize, using the min-cut algorithm, an energy function that considers various features such as: temporal color similarity, spatial color continuity and spatial motion continuity. The obtained results are compared to those obtained by other relevant works such as: mean-shift tracker [59] and

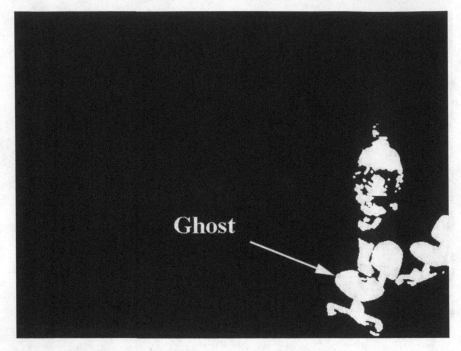

Ghost

Fig. 3.8 The result of the object detection algorithm applied to the frame shown in Fig. 3.7

"FragTrack" [60]. Figure 3.11 is extracted from [57] and it shows the results obtained in the comparative evaluation of the aforementioned methods applied to the "car sequence" (an image sequence extracted from the VIVID database [61]).

- **Articulated shape and skeletal models**: the algorithms falling in this category try to represent the object shape using a model of interconnected geometrical primitive (such as ellipse and/or rectangle for contour and segments for the skeletal models). For example, in [62] the human body is modeled by means of a puppet composed of 9 interconnected rectangle (one for torso, two for each arm and two for each leg) while in [63] has been proposed also a skeletal models.

After the object representation has been chosen, it still remains the problem of tracking the objects through the various frames. The model selected to represent the recognized objects has a strong influence on the method used for tracking them. For example, translational models are used to track objects represented by a point while affine or projective transformations are used to track objects represented by means of ellipses or rectangles. As said above, this kind of representation is able to model the motion of rigid objects in the scene. For non-rigid objects, the most frequently used object representations are silhouettes or contours and their motions are modeled by means of both parametric and non-parametric models.

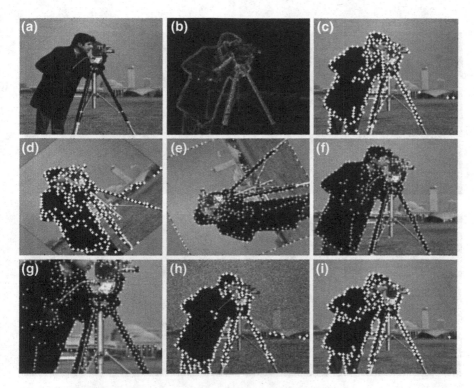

Fig. 3.9 a Original image, **b** Local frequency image, **c** Extracted feature points. Feature points detected in rotated images for **d** 45°, **e** 115°. Feature points detected in images for the scaling **f** 1.2, **g** 2. Feature points detected in noisy images for the SNR **h** 19 dB and **i** 40 dB [45] (reproduced by permission of IEEE)

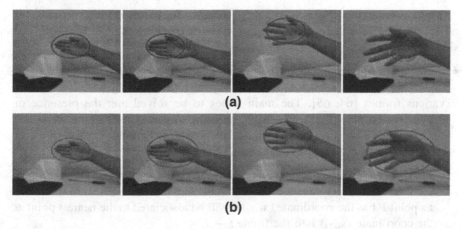

Fig. 3.10 A comparative evaluation between the results obtained in [51] (**a**) and those obtained in [46] (**b**); (reproduced by permission of IEEE)

(a)

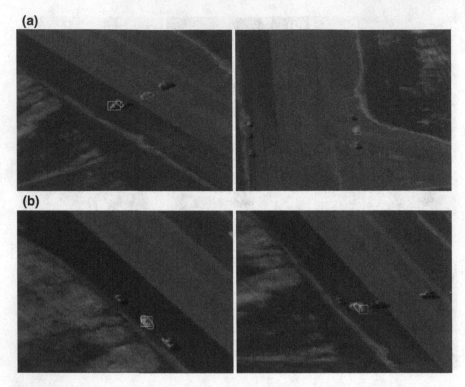

(b)

Fig. 3.11 This figure shows the results of a comparative evaluation between the method proposed in [57] (*half transparent green figure*) and other relevant methods: mean-shift tracker (*red ellipse*), "FragTrack" (*yellow rectangle*). The latter two methods lose the car already before frame #600 (reproduced by permission of IEEE)

Starting from these considerations, it is possible to divide the methods for object tracking into three main categories: **point tracking**, **kernel tracking** and **silhouette tracking**.

- **Point tracking**: the methods falling into this category face the problem of finding the correspondence of detected objects represented by points across the various frames [64, 65]. The main issues to be solved are: the presence of occlusions, erroneous detections, the appearing of new objects in the scene and the exits of old objects. Many methods are based on the minimization of a cost function based on some physical constraints such as:

  - **proximity**: according to this constraint, the position of a point can not vary too much between two consecutive frames. In this framework, if in the frame t a point P has the coordinate (x_t, y_t) it will be associated to the nearest point at the coordinate (x_t, y_t) into the frame $t + 1$.
  - **maximum velocity**: assumes that the speed of the moving objects has a reasonable limit that can vary according to the various applications.

- **small velocity change**: considers the fact that typically, object speed varies smoothly between neighborhood frames.
- **common motion**: this constrain is used for tracking complex rigid objects represented by more than one point. Since the object is rigid, the speed of its representative points should be almost the same.
- **rigidity**: starting from the same principle of the previous one, this constraint works on the distance rather than on the speed.
- **combination** of two or more of the previous constraints.

- **Kernel tracking:** the methods falling into this category try to compute the motion of the moving objects tracking a primitive object region frame by frame [66, 67]. Typically they are used to model translational motion and/or affine transformations. The various methods differ among them in terms of: number of tracked objects, motion models and method used to represent the object appearance.
- **Silhouette tracking:** into this category there are all the methods trying to track the object silhouette [68, 69]. There are moving objects that are composed of multiple sub-parts in relative motion among them. A common example of such a moving object can be a walking man. In this kind of video the "complex moving object" is the walking man and its sub-parts are head, torso, arms and legs. Since the appearance of such kind of moving objects changes among the various frames, the methods for silhouette tracking try to identify the silhouette in a given frame using an object's model built analyzing the previous frames. For which it may concern the case of human tracking, it is a research field drawing significant attention due to the large number of potential applications. There are various models of the human body according to the various system settings. Typically, 2D models [70] are used in systems based on un-calibrated monocular cameras, while, 3D models [71] are more popular in stereo-system and/or multi-camera settings. An interesting survey of the approaches proposed in literature to perform this task is [72].

3.5 Human Behavior Analysis and Recognition

Human behavior analysis and recognition: This is one of the most challenging tasks for the international researchers' community. Here the problem of the semantic gap must be faced to obtain satisfying results. Furthermore, the errors done at the earlier stages have strong effects here (for example, the object tracking module can lose a person due to an occlusion while this person is performing an interesting act for the behavior analysis application).

In various works, terms like actions, activities, complex or simple actions, and behaviors are often used in an undifferentiated way. This fact makes their comparison and/or classification difficult. In this book the following action hierarchy is used: action primitives, actions, and activities. At the highest level of the hierarchy there are the activities (for example dancing), each activity is composed of a set of actions (for example: pirouette, etc.) and each action is in turn divided into action primitives (the set of sequential elementary steps to perform to do a pirouette). The works presented in this chapter are classified according to the following visual abstraction hierarchy:

- **scene interpretation**: these works try to interpret the whole image without identifying particular objects or humans;
- **human recognition**: where either the entire human body or individual body parts are identified and used for the recognition task
- **action primitives and grammars**: these works try to obtain a semantic description of the scene starting from the identification of an action hierarchy.

3.5.1 Scene Interpretation

The works falling in this framework try to interpret the whole scene. The moving objects are detected and tracked without considering their identity (they can be humans or other moving objects). Typically, these systems have two working stages:

- **Learning stage**: where the observed trajectories of the moving objects are classified using various methods to build the system knowledge base. This stage is not trivial because human motion is highly non-linear, a priori unknown, and it is always subject to sudden and unforeseeable changes of orientation and speed;
- **Operating stage**: where the knowledge base is used to classify the runtime observed object trajectories.

These systems are used in frameworks where a well defined set of situations are allowed while others are forbidden or in applications where the goal is to classify the scenes/behaviors in usual or unusual. At this level of visual abstraction, the moving objects are considered in their completeness. This allows for building systems that analyze at a high level the objects trajectories and their interactions.

The main drawbacks of the works falling in this class are:

- They produce a poor semantic level analysis of the scene: indeed, they are only able to state if a given behavior is usual or unusual or in other words if a scene is known or unknown
- The number of recognizable actions is limited to that of the actions learnt in the learning stage. Furthermore, this stage is not trivial due to issues cited above.

In literature there are many works using this approach.

In [73] an approach is proposed to classify scenes in usual and unusual ones by starting from the analysis of a single frame or object rather than from a sequence of frames. This method is tested in various environments both indoor and outdoor. It is designed to work on huge datasets, indeed, the results presented in the paper are obtained on a database composed of 4 years of continuous video acquisition (that give millions of records). Despite the fact that this work is quite old, it still remains a key work because it represents clearly the potentiality of the methods using scene interpretation.

They use an advanced motion detection method modeling the background as a Gaussian mixture [31]. The detected moving objects are described by means of a feature vector composed of: position, dimension, speed, moving direction and a binary representation of the object silhouette. The feature space is quantized with an online vector quantization method to obtain a codebook (namely a set of prototype representations which approximate the density of the input representations). This method starts selecting K random prototypes among the existing data. Then, each point in the dataset is associated to the nearest prototype that is adapted toward the data point using a learning factor. Some constraints from [74] are applied to avoid the problems that occur when an outlier is selected as initial prototype. After the codebook has been generated, it is used in all the successive classification processes instead of the whole original dataset obtaining a strong improvement in the classification performance in terms of processing time.

Since this system works by classifying a single object and or a single frame rather than recognizing sequences, it considers a sequence as a multi-set of symbols. A multi-set is a set that can contain multiple instances of the same element. Each pair of objects in a sequence belonging to the same multi-set is evidence that those two prototypes' appearances resulted from the same underlying class. The multi-sets of prototypes are used to estimate the co-occurrence statistic over the codebook. All the prototypes and the co-occurrence matrix defined on them are used to define a binary tree structure by recursively defining two probability mass functions across the prototypes of the code book that best explain the co-occurrence matrix. The leaf nodes of the binary tree are probability distributions of co-occurrences across the prototypes and at a higher tree depth define simple scene activities like pedestrian and car movement. These can then be used for scene interpretation. The proposed results are obtained testing the system on a streaming video recording a scene that consists of a road with adjacent parking spots and a path through the grass near the loading bay of a building. The camera is placed far from the scene so that the moving objects appear to be quite small.

The strong points of this method are:

- **The tracking method** is based on a Gaussian mixture model of the background that has been proven to be quite reliable also in outdoor scenes because it is able to model the slight changes in luminosity. The same is not valid for sudden changes due, for example, to the car's headlight in the night. Nevertheless, the system can work also at night because the scene is taken from far and a car with headlight turned-on occupies a small percentage of the frame.
- **The ability to handle huge datasets**. The used concept of "codebook" can be ideally considered as a "summary" of the all recorded scenes. This approach is often used also in other fields of applications, such as in image database

indexing [75, 76] to speed up the search process in complex database. Using this technique is useful also for the successive step of co-occurrence statistic definition and it introduce a strong improvement in the system performance. The key element of this approach is the size of the codebook. A codebook with many elements can be used to classify more actions but the needed data to build the co-occurrence statistic accumulation on it grows-up as the square of its dimension. This point can become a limit to the applicability of this system in frameworks with a great variance in the performable actions.

- **The ability to recognize an action starting from few instances of objects**. In this work, the authors propose an instance classifier rather than a sequence classifier. This result is obtained considering each single observation in a sequence as an independent one both in the stage of codebook generation and in that of co-occurrence statistic definition. Once again, the codebook is a key element. If the codebook elements are able to describe in an unambiguous manner each instance, the system will work but, if the operative framework becomes more complex and the number of elements in the codebook becomes insufficient to describe in an unambiguous manner each instance, the system will not work very fine.

A second class of approaches for detecting anomalies in video sequences and/or in single images has been proposed in [77]. This method tries to decompose the normal (or the allowed) video sequences and/or images in small multi-scale portions defining the knowledge base of the system. When the system analyzes a query video and/or image, it tries to rebuild the query using the portions stored in the knowledge base. The regions of the query that can be rebuilt using large portions from the database are considered as "normal" while those that can not be rebuilt or that can be rebuilt using small and fragmented portions are regarded as "suspicious".

The single images are decomposed in a set of spatial multi-scale portions. Each portion is described by means of a feature vector considering its absolute position in the image and a synthetic representation of the gradient of each its pixel. A video sequence is decomposed in spatial–temporal multi-scale portions. The feature vector describing each portion reports its absolute position and the absolute values of the temporal derivatives in all pixels of the portion.

In order to speed-up the image/video rebuilding process and thus the whole interpretation task, the authors propose an inference method based on a probabilistic analysis of the portions allowing for small local misalignments in their relative geometric arrangement. This approach allows for a rapid and efficient detection of subtle but important local changes in behavior.

The main drawbacks of this method are:

- **Computational complexity**: the examples reported in the work are relative to single images and short video sequences. The inference process is quite efficient, but the database can become very "heavy" when long video sequences are analyzed.

- **The feature vector used to describe the portions**: as the same authors say, the used feature vector is quite simple, but the proposed system is modular and so it could be able to use other features. The computer vision research community has elaborated more sophisticated descriptors.
- **Probabilistic analysis**: this is the kernel of the inference process (because the entire task of similarity computation among portions is based on it) and perhaps the most limitative drawback of this system. This analysis is based on an assumption that is almost never applicable in real situations: there are not overlapping areas among the portions. This assumption is necessary to compute the similarity between pairs of portions, but it makes this system unsuitable in each situation where there are partial occlusions among moving objects.

A third class of approaches is based on the study of the trajectories of the moving objects and focuses the attention both on the geometric characteristics of the trajectories and on their cinematic aspects. The idea standing at the base of these works is that in a given place, similar trajectories can be associated to similar activities. In this way, analyzing and classifying the trajectories described by a moving object is equivalent to analyze and classify its activities.

Reference [78] proposes a method to distinguish between objects traversing spatially dissimilar paths, or objects traversing spatially proximal paths but having different spatial–temporal characteristics.

The system uses a fixed camera and a tracker to record the trajectories of the moving objects. A recursive min-cut clustering algorithm is used to group similar trajectories. The distance between two trajectories is computed using the Hausdorff distance. This fact allows the system to compute the distance between two trajectories composed of a different number of points. To limit the spatial extent of a path, an envelope is defined using a dynamic time warping algorithm.

The system performs a hierarchical classification using different features at each level. The first level uses only the geometric properties of the trajectory. If a given trajectory is not geometrically similar to any in the database, it is considered "unusual". If a given trajectory is similar to one in the database, the second stage classification is performed. The second level works on the cinematic properties of the trajectories thus evaluating the velocities of the moving objects. The third level analyzes the discontinuity in the trajectories. The system analyzes the discontinuity in speed, acceleration and curvature. This criterion is able to detect irregular motion patterns that can be associated to particular situation (i.e., a drunk man walking).

From a conceptual point of view, this work has good performances. The problems arise when this system analyzes crowded scenes. Indeed, in this situation, the tracker is not able to track all the moving objects (due to the mutual occlusions) and so it is difficult to associate a trajectory to each moving object. Actually, this problem is common almost in all the works in the research field on human behavior analysis because it is the result of the propagation of an error occurring in a lower level of the computational pyramid shown in Fig. 3.1 (object tracking module).

While the ratio behind the association of semantic meaning to the object trajectories is a common point to all the works falling in this framework (scene interpretation), there are sensible differences in the method used to detect, model and handle the object trajectories.

For example, in [79] the authors use non-rigid shapes and a dynamic model that characterizes the variations in the shape structure. This system is specialized in surveillance task where it is important to discriminate between "normal" and "abnormal" behaviors. The authors propose a method to model the shape of group of simultaneously moving objects that in the surveillance framework means to model the activities of group of people.

They use the Dryden and Mardia's statistical shape theory [80] to represent the shape of the configuration of a group of moving objects and its deformations over time. In other words, they model a trajectory activity as a mean stationary trajectory plus a set of allowed deformations due to slight difference on the paths followed by the various moving objects and/or to the displacement among the various moving objects following the same path.

This method represents a pragmatic solution to the problem of occlusions in crowded scenes. The ratio behind this solution is: since it is not possible (at least till today and in a perfect way) to detect and track each moving object in a crowded scene, we try to model and characterize the motion of the whole crowd.

This approach has perfect sense in video surveillance systems applied to particular operative context such as transit areas in airports and stations where it is possible to classify the possible paths in common/allowed paths and reserved/ forbidden paths.

In [81] the authors propose a system having the same ratio and application framework of the previous one (video surveillance) but a different way to model the shapes. Here they are described as the composition of basis shapes obtained by applying the factorization theorem [82] to the 3D shape that can be recovered from the motion tracks of points in a 2D image sequence.

A different approach is proposed in [83]. Here, the concept of object trajectory is leaved and an activity is represented as a succession of basic events and modeled through interpretation of the temporal and causal correlations among different classes of events. An event is defined as a group of significant changes in pixels in a local image neighborhood over the time. The events are detected and classified by unsupervised clustering using Gaussian Mixture Model with automatic model selection based on Schwarz's Bayesian Information Criterion [84]. A robust and holistic scene-level behavior interpretation method is implemented using Dynamic Probabilistic Networks to model the temporal and causal correlations among discrete events.

This approach is quite different from the others presented in this section. It leaves both the concept of object detection and that of trajectory. In this way the problem of occlusions is not considered because the system tries to model the behavior of the entire group of moving (and self-occluding) objects. According to the experimental results presented by the authors, this system is suitable to model different situations such as: aircraft cargo loading/unloading activities and shopping activities.

The main drawbacks of this work are:

- It requires a large training set to model complex situations
- Since it does not attempt to track each moving object (trying to resolve the problem of partial occlusions occurring in crowded scene) in a scene, it is not able to evaluate what happens among the elements of the moving group. For this reason it is not suitable in mission critical security systems.

3.5.2 Human Recognition

The works falling in this class try to infer information about the human beings activities analyzing the dynamic of their movements. Some of these works try to recognize and study the motion of the individual body parts while others consider the whole body as a unique element.

The works falling in this class produce a motion analysis with a semantic level richer than that obtained by the works belonging to the scene interpretation class. Indeed, while the latter are able to classify a scene/behavior as known or unknown, the former works try to identify elementary actions such as walk, running, the human gait but also more complex actions when applied in a narrow domain (for example the actions of a tennis match in [85]).

Also these works are characterized by a learning stage and an operative stage and so, also for these works the number of recognizable actions is limited to that of the actions learnt in the learning stage.

Furthermore, since these works try to analyze the single action with a fine level of detail, the execution speed of the various movements and hence the sampling rate of the camera can become critical parameters. A direct consequence of this fact is the difficulty in delimiting the action in the operating stage.

An example of work considering the whole body as a unique element is [86]. Here the authors consider videos where the human beings are tall about 30 pixels (they call this situation "medium field" while they define "far field" the scenes where human beings are tall about 3 pixels and "near field" those where they are tall 300 pixels). They motivate this choice considering that this is the classical resolution of many videos of sport events where people can easily track individual players and recognize actions such as running, kicking, jumping (despite the small dimension of the players). Each moving person is tracked so that the image is stabilized in the middle of a tracking window. This removes the effects of the absolute motion of the tracked person in the scene (it is equivalent to the panning movement by a camera operator who keeps the moving figure in the centre of the field of view). In this way, any residual motion within the spatio-temporal volume is due to the relative motions of different body parts: limbs, head, torso etc., The analysis of these residual motions is at the base of this method. Given a stabilized figure-centric sequence, the optical flow is computed and decomposed into two scalar fields corresponding to the horizontal and vertical components of the optical flow. These fields are decomposed into four non negative channels. Each channel is blurred with a Gaussian and normalized to obtain the final descriptor for the image sequence.

According to the authors, this system has a good performance in terms of sequences recognition. It works onto scenes recorded in the "medium field" maximizing the information in the blurred areas due to the residual motion. The critical points can be:

- the system is able to recognize similar sequences also if they are recorded with slight different frame rates, but the system is not able to analyze sequences of different lengths.
- the length of the motion descriptors (i.e., the number of frames used to analyze an action) can be a critical parameter. Indeed, it is a constant value fixed at design time. From this point of view, the system is not able to recognize the same action performed at two different speeds.

A hierarchical approach is proposed in [85] where a system for human behavior analysis in the narrow domain (tennis match) is presented. Here, a given human behavior is considered as composed of a stochastic sequence of actions. Actions are described by a feature vector comprising both trajectory information (position and velocity), and a set of local motion descriptors. The used local motion descriptors are an advanced version of those used in [86]. Indeed, the coarse optical flow descriptor used in [86] has been endowed with data about the position where a given action is performed. Action recognition is achieved by means of a probabilistic search method applied to the database representing previously seen actions. The possible actions are modeled by means of Hidden Markov Models (HMM): high-level behavior recognition is achieved by computing the likelihood that a set of predefined Hidden Markov Models explains the current action sequence. Thus, human actions and behavior are represented using a hierarchy of abstraction: from simple actions, to actions with spatio-temporal context, to action sequences and finally general behaviors. This system has been used to produce high semantic level video annotations for tennis matches.

The main drawbacks of this work are:

- the high dimensionality of the feature space: according to the authors, "there are 30,000 entries in a single local motion feature vector for a 30×50 pixel target". Even thought the authors propose a solution to this problem (a database structured as a binary tree via principal component analysis of the data set), it can become a restriction for using this approach in more complex scenarios;
- this system is not able to generalize knowledge about the recorded scenes. Indeed, it is able to recognize and label a given action using a fixed knowledge base created during the learning stage.

Other approaches are based on the concept of "temporal templates" (a static vector-image where the vector value at each point is a function of the motion properties at the corresponding spatial location in an image sequence). This idea was proposed in [87] where the authors used a two components version of the templates: the first value is a binary value indicating the presence of motion and the second value is a function of the recency of motion in a sequence. These components are called MEI (Motion-Energy Image) and MHI (Motion-History Image) respectively. MEIs are cumulative binary motion images, namely, binary images where the value of each pixel is set to 0 if its value does not change for each frame of a given sequence (namely, no moving objects have passed over it) while it is set to 1 otherwise. MHIs are grey scale images where pixel intensity is a function of the temporal history of motion at that point. In these images, the more recently moving pixels are brighter. From a certain point of view, considering a given scene, the MEI image describes *where* the motion occurs while the MHI describes *how* it occurs. Matching temporal templates is based on Hu moments [88].

The main limit of this approach is its dependency by the speed of the action and by the frame rate. Indeed, the same action executed at different speed or recorded with different frame rates, gives different MHI and MEI.

A variant of the concept of MHI is called *timed MHI* (tMHI) and is presented in [89]. This method tries to overcome the limit of the previous approach due to its dependence by the frame rate and/or execution time. In order to obtain this result, the authors use the timestamp and introduce a limit into the duration of an action (a constant of few seconds). In this way, a given gesture will cover the same MHI area at different capture rates.

Another approach is that of "Actions Sketches" or "Space–Time Shapes" in the 3D XYT volume. In [90] the authors propose to model an action based on both the shape and the motion of the object performing the action. When the object performs an action in 3D, the points on the outer boundary of the object are projected as 2D (x, y) contour in the image plane. A sequence of such 2D contours with respect to time generates a spatiotemporal volume (STV) in (x, y, t), which can be treated as 3D object in the (x, y, t) space. The differential geometric surface properties of this 3D object (such as peaks, pits, valleys and ridges) are considered specific action descriptors capturing both spatial and temporal properties. For example, a pit surface is generated when the contour first moves in the direction that is normal to the contour, then stops and moves in the opposite direction.

Instead of using spatio-temporal volumes, a large number of papers choose the more classical approach of considering sequences of silhouettes. For example, in [91], the authors present a method for human motion pattern recognition based on Principal Component Analysis (PCA) and neural networks. They extract the silhouettes of the moving objects in the various frames. Each 2D silhouette contour is converted into a one dimensional signal computing the distance between each point of the silhouette contour and its barycenter. The PCA is used to reduce the dimension of the feature space (using 32 components to describe each silhouette, the 96 % of variance is retained) and a three layers neural network has been trained to recognize the *walking*, *running* and *other* actions.

In a number of publications, recognition is based on HMMs and Dynamic Bayes Networks (DBNs).

For example, in [92], the authors present an object-based system for video analysis and interpretation. The basic unit for analysis is the video object (VO), a concept introduced by MPEG-4. Instead of considering as basic unit of analysis the whole frame, in this approach the low-level features from individual objects in the frames (VO) are considered. From extracted VOs, they followed a pattern analysis methodology by modeling the VO behavior using DBNs, which can generate a hierarchical description for the video events. They showed that the object-based approach is effective for a complete characterization of video sequences, which includes both macro-grained and fine-grained semantics contained in the video sequences.

According to the authors, a serious limitation of this approach is that the description generated by DBNs is very fine-grained. It works the best for simple video events. But for long video sequences involving various video events, this approach is unlikely to be satisfactory.

Unsupervised methods (such as HMMs) can be trained automatically but yield models whose internal structure—the nodes—are difficult to interpret semantically. Manually constructed networks typically have nodes corresponding to sub-events, but the programming and training of these networks is tedious and requires extensive domain expertise. In [93] the authors propose a semi-supervised approach where a manually structured, Propagation Network (a form of a DBN) is initialized from a small amount of fully annotated data, and then refined by an Expectation Maximization based learning method in an unsupervised fashion. During node refinement (the M step) a boosting-based algorithm is employed to train the evidence detectors of individual nodes. The proposed results shown that, starting from few full annotated example accompanied by a small number of positive but non-annotated training examples, the system can achieve good performance in indoor activity analysis and also in other applications.

In literature there are also many works attempting to infer information about human behaviors analyzing the dynamics and settings of the individual body parts. After they have recognized the position of the various body parts, it is possible to consider some constraints and extract some features that can be indicative of some specific actions/behaviors.

For example, in [94] the authors consider three dynamic regularity features. They are temporal properties and are generally independent of camera position:

- **Cycle Time**: this time is referred to the cycle time of a leg which decreases with increasing walking speed. It is computed by measuring the time interval between two successive minima or maxima in the trajectory of a foot.
- **Stance/Swing Ratio**: *stance time* is the period of time when the foot is in contact with the ground while the *swing time* is the period of time when the foot is not in contact with the ground. The ratio stance/swing decreases when a person walks faster.
- **Double Support Time**: this is the period of time when both feet are in contact with the ground. This occurs twice in the gait cycle, at the beginning and end of the stance phase.

Using these features, the authors are able to distinguish walking examples across multiple speeds from other non-walking actions.

A critical element for this kind of systems is the fact that they are substantially view dependent also if the dynamic regularities features that they use are not view dependent.

An attempting to create a view invariant system has been done in [95]. Here the authors, starting from the findings in [96] (where the authors developed relationships between six-tuple 3D points and their corresponding image coordinates that are satisfied for all views of the 3D points), propose a 3D approach aiming for viewpoint invariance. Each action is represented as a unique curve in a 3D invariance-space, surrounded by an acceptance volume ('action-volume'). The "action-volume" concept derives from the experimental observation of the fact that each person performing more than one time the same task produces curves in the 3D invariance-space that are slightly different among them. To take into account these "slightly" differences, the authors consider an "acceptance-volume" surrounding the mean 3D curve describing the action and they call this volume "action-volume". Given a video sequence, 2D quantities from each frame are calculated and matched against candidate action volumes in a probabilistic framework.

As the results presented by the authors show, this approach has encouraging results, but it is far from the goal of a full view-independent system. Indeed, a constraint of this approach is that at least 4 of the 6 3D points representing the "invariant" must lie on different planes. After the designer chooses the six points on a person, it is possible that, for a given view-point, they do not satisfy this constraint (according to the instantaneous pose) and so, for that view-point, the performance decreases.

Another approach to view-independent system has been proposed in [97] where the authors propose an approach to matching human actions that is both fully descriptive in terms of motion and is both invariant to view and execution rate. They use a point-based representation of the human body. In particular, each point represents the spatial coordinate of an anatomical landmark on the human body. A central point of this work is the fact that it uses the statistical results about the proportion among the various human body parts described in [98] to introduce geometric constraints among the points representing a human body. In this way they are able to recognize a given action also if it was carried out by different people. Since it is expected that different people may perform some portions of the same action at different rates, the dynamic time warp was used to make this approach invariant to the different execution rates.

According to the authors, this system can achieve good results but it was tested only in particular conditions where, for example, there were not occlusions.

3.5.3 Action Primitive and Grammars

Works falling into this class attempt to decouple actions into action primitives and to interpret actions as a composition on the alphabet of these action primitives.

Some of the works falling in this class still use a learning based approach and so they are able only to recognize the learnt actions but in this class there are also works using a generative approach [99] and works starting without any models [100]. In this way it is possible to overcome the limit intrinsic to the learning stage. Also for this class of works the video sampling rate can be a critical parameter for the same reasons seen for the previous class.

Due to the fine level of observation of the scene, the performances of these works are heavily influenced by the noise and the occlusion problems.

A method employing techniques from the dynamical systems framework is presented in [101] where the authors propose to decompose a human activity into a set of elementary actions. These elementary actions can be seen as symbols of an "alphabet" and so, they can be used to describe human motions similar to the way phonemes are used in speech. They call these primitives of motion "movemes". By using system identification techniques and pattern recognition techniques they develop an on-line joint segmentation and classification algorithm and provide analytical error analysis. After the primitives are detected, an iterative approach is used to find the sequence of primitives for a novel action.

The authors show the results obtained using the system to describe the movements carried out by five different people that are drawing a set of shapes using a computer mouse.

The ratio behind this approach is very interesting because this system proposes a "generative" approach to the human behavior analysis. The main drawback of this work is that it is quite difficult to apply it in real live situations where problems of noise and occlusions occur.

Another approach from the system theoretic point of view is presented in [102] where the authors try to segment and represent repetitive movements. They use a two-threshold multidimensional segmentation algorithm to automatically decompose a complex motion into a sequence of simple linear dynamic models (second order AR models). The problem of action segmentation is resolved in terms of model changes. Namely, the motion segmentation problem is solved detecting the times at which the dynamical parameters of the AR model used to describe the current action change significantly. No a priori assumptions were made about the number of models that comprise the full motion or about the duration of the task cycle. A compact motion representation is obtained for each segment using parameters of a damped harmonic dynamic model.

The main drawback of this system is the fact that it is able to segment and recognize variations of motions known to the classifier. This fact diminishes the generality of this approach making it usable only in tasks where repetitive motions are present. Furthermore, according to the authors, this system is not suitable for real-time analysis.

A vision based approach is proposed in [100] where the authors propose to describe human actions in terms of *action units* called "dynamic instants" and "intervals" which can be computed studying the spatio-temporal curvature of a 2-D trajectory. The *dynamic instants* are due to changes in the forces applied to the object during the activity. They are perceived as a change in the direction and/or speed and can be reliably detected by identifying maxima in the spatio-temporal curvature of the action trajectory. An *interval* is the period of time between two dynamic instants during which the motion characteristics do not change. The authors formally show that the *dynamic instants* are view-invariant, except in the limited cases of accidental alignment. The rationale behind this approach has a psychological root in works such as [103–105]. The authors focus their attention on human actions performed by a hand. Examples of such actions are: opening and closing overhead cabinets, picking up and putting down a book, picking up and putting down a phone, erasing a white-board, etc. Starting without a model, they use this representation for recognition and incremental learning of human actions. The system tracks the hand using a skin detector algorithm. According to the authors, the proposed method can discover instances of the same action performed by different people from different view points. In the experimental section are shown results on 47 actions performed by 7 individuals in an environment with no constraints obtaining good performances in terms of action recognition.

This approach presents various interesting aspects such as:

- it starts without a predefined model of the actions to be recognized and this, as discussed above, is a desirable characteristic for this kind of systems.
- it is "almost" view invariant because it is able to recognize the same action recorded from different view points. The term "almost" view invariant refers to the fact that it fails in recognizing actions performed on a plane perpendicular to the view plane.

On the other hand, the main drawback of this system is related to the required sample rate. Indeed, since the system recognizes *dynamic instants* studying the spatio-temporal properties of the hand's trajectory (it searches for the maxima in the spatio-temporal curvature of the action trajectory), it requires a detailed representation of this curve. In other words, it must use an adequate sampling rate to sample this curve. This sampling rate varies in a proportional way to the speed at which a given action is performed. Having a low sampling rate, it is possible to lose some *dynamic instants* reducing the performance of the whole system.

In literature it is possible to find also systems attempting to achieve a higher semantic level analysis of the human behaviors in the recorded scenes.

For example, in [106] the authors propose a system performing a hierarchical analysis of a video stream. The lowest level analyzes the poses of individual body parts including head, torso, arms and legs are recognized using individual Bayesian networks (BNs), which are then integrated to obtain an overall body pose. The middle level models the activity of a single person using a dynamic Bayesian network (DBN). The higher level of the hierarchy works on the results of the mid-level layer. Here, the descriptions for each person are juxtaposed along a common time line to identify an interaction between two persons. According to the authors, the following nine interaction types are considered in this paper: the neutral interactions include (1) approaching each other, (2) departing each other, and (3) pointing, and the positive interactions include (4) shaking hands, (5) hugging, and (6) standing hand-in-hand, and the negative interactions include (7) punching, (8) pushing, and (9) kicking.

An interesting aspect of this work is the high semantic level of its output. Indeed, according to the authors, the human action is automatically represented in terms of verbal description according to subject + verb + object syntax, and human interaction is represented in terms of cause + effect semantics between the human actions.

The main drawbacks of this system are:

- the method used to classify the interaction between two people: indeed this task is accomplished using a decision tree. This fact makes this system suitable for recognizing a well defined and fixed set of interactions (the nine listed above);
- as a direct consequence of the previous point, the system is not able to generalize the observed behaviors. Hence, it is not able to recognize interactions that do not belong to the training set and so, for example, it is not able to recognize actions where more than two people are involved.
- Occlusions: the whole hierarchy is based on the principle that the system is able to identify the single body parts of the people in the scene. In this way, for example, at the middle level it is possible to infer information about the pose of a man. This is a critical point because in this kind of systems, there are both self-occlusions and mutual occlusions among people.

Working on the same concept of multi level analysis, where at the lower levels the action primitives are recognized and sent at the higher levels to perform a more complex analysis, in [99] the authors propose to use a Stochastic Context Free Grammar (SCFG) to obtain a high semantic level analysis of human behavior. In this work, the authors propose a probabilistic approach to the analysis of temporally extended actions encompassing also the problem of interactions among moving objects. The system is composed of two levels. The first level detects action primitives using standard independent probabilistic event detectors to propose candidate detections of low-level features. The outputs of these detectors are sent as input stream to the second level. Here a stochastic context-free grammar parsing mechanism is used to analyze the stream and perform a higher semantic level analysis. The main advantages of this approach are that it provides longer range temporal constraints, disambiguates uncertain low-level detections, and allows the inclusion of a priori knowledge about the structure of temporal events in a given domain.

An interesting aspect of this method is the use of the grammar as a convenient means for encoding the external knowledge about the problem domain, expressing the expected structure of the activity.

The main limit of this approach is the fact that it uses low-level features detectors that are able to model and recognize only a fixed number of action primitives.

An interesting aspect of the human behavior and of his communicative capacity is the gestural expressiveness. In literature, a large number of works, dealing with the human gesture analysis, are present. This problem can be seen as particular case of the human behavior analysis.

Many video-based methods have been developed for hand [107], arm [108] and full-body [109] gesture recognition. These systems can be classified in the following classes according to the methodology of analysis that they use:

- landmark based: these systems detect and track some landmarks such as body parts [110], "visual interesting points" [111], "visual cues" [108] or "feature points" [109].
- kinematical based: in these systems, movement kinematical parameters related to the articulated body motion are first recovered as joint-angle vectors or body-centered joint locations. Action recognition is then conducted in such kinematical parameter spaces [99, 112]. It should be noticed as this kind of representation of the human body parts is the same used in many works cited above.
- template based: these systems represent actions using image information such as silhouettes or 3D volumetric reconstruction such as visual hulls. These systems can be further divided into two classes according to the method that they use for feature extraction and action recognition:
- holistic approaches [113, 114]: these systems model the entire action as a spatio-temporal shape. The recognition task is accomplished comparing this model with a set of learnt models using statistical pattern recognition techniques such as SVM, LDA.
- sequential approaches [115, 116]: these systems represent an action as a temporal series of key poses. In the training phase, a set of key poses are first selected from the gesture set. Each key pose is described by means of a features vector often called "pose feature vector". Action recognition is then achieved through sequential pattern recognition using methods such as hidden Markov models (HMM) and/or Bayesian networks.

3.6 Summary

In this section, an introduction to the problem of human behavior analysis in video streaming has been presented showing an overview of the main works on this topic present in literature.

These works follow a well defined and accepted processing chain as shown in Fig. 3.1. This fact introduces a hierarchical decomposition of this problem into various modules allowing the researchers for focusing their attention on specific aspects of the problem. Following this principle, the object of this book is the definition of an innovative methodology to implement systems for high semantic level analysis of human behavior in streaming video recorded into the narrow domain. For this reason, this literature overview considers only the works falling in the highest level of the processing chain showed in Fig. 3.1 (namely human behavior analysis and recognition).

These works can be divided into three main classes according to the aspect of the problem that they consider (whole scene, whole human body and single body parts).

This research topic has attracted many researchers in the last years due to the large number of potential applications in various fields (surveillance, control, analysis). Despite the efforts of scientific community, automatic high semantic level analysis of video streaming still remain a problem far to be solved. This is due to the lack of a comprehensive and universally valid solution to two problems: semantic and sensory gaps. For this reason, in literature it is possible to find many works dealing with specific aspects of the problem and providing satisfying solutions in well defined operating conditions.

One of the most widely accepted assumptions by the works on this topic is the processing chain. Indeed, using this processing chain it is possible to decompose the general problem (semantic human behavior analysis) into various aspects. In this way, it is possible to face these aspects singularly without considering the whole problem. So, it is possible to build hierarchical systems where the output of the module of a given level becomes the input for the module at the successive level (see Fig. 3.1).

As shown in this literature overview this approach has some drawbacks. Indeed, often the performances of the higher level modules are affected by the errors done to the lower levels. Another open issue to be faced is the definition of an effective representation of the observed scene. This representation should reach an adequate level of detail for all the semantic processes to be implemented. On the other hands, it should be as compact as possible to avoid problems related to the computational complexity.

Many works attempt to recognize human activity using statistical approaches and searching the query action in a knowledge base composed of a set of recognizable activities. This approach can give good results in some scenarios, but it has an intrinsic limit: it is not able to recognize actions that do not belong to the knowledge base (and hence to the training set used to create it). On the other hand, the idea to define "generative" approaches to the human behavior analysis has been used in various works. They attempt to recognize a complex activity using the composition of elementary and recognizable actions.

Recognizing activities is an extremely complicated task at which even humans are often less than perfect. The implementation of an automatic system performing this task is an open research field. As shown in this chapter, in literature, some works achieving good results in recognizing specific human activities are present. But the trend is quite clear: the higher is the required semantic level analysis the narrower must be the domain of application.

In this book, a methodological approach to implement systems for high semantic analysis of video streaming is proposed. The key issues faced by this methodology are:

- **sensory gap**: since, as shown above, the errors done at the lower level of the processing chain can influence the performance of the semantic analysis, in this book an innovative method to reduce the sensory gap is proposed. This method reduces the problem of occlusions among moving objects using a multi-camera approach. The details of this method are shown in Chap. 4.
- **model representation**: the proposed methodology represents the actions using string of symbols. In this way it is possible to obtain a compact representation suitable for real time analysis. The details of this method are shown in Chap. 5.
- **semantic gap**: the proposed methodology works in narrow domains exploiting some background knowledge about scene and/or the human behavior, thus narrowing the huge variety of possible behavioral patterns by focusing on a specific narrow domain. A linguistic approach based on the definition of a specific grammar for each domain is used to obtain a high semantic level analysis of human behavior. The details of this method are shown in Chap. 5.

Chapter 4
Sensor Data Interpretation for Symbolic Analysis

This chapter describes an original contribute of this book: a method to solve the correspondence problem in multi-camera systems without the assumption of epipolar geometry [117, 118]. This method is suitable to reduce the sensory gap and the problem of the presence of mutual occlusions among moving objects inside a scene. Using this method it is possible to improve the performance of the tracking algorithm. The chapter starts with a brief problem overview and then it presents a description of the epipolar geometry. Finally the proposed solution is described and the final considerations are reported.

4.1 Introduction

As seen, in the previous chapter, many approaches to human behavior analysis work by studying the trajectories of some relevant points. These systems have good performances but they all fail when the motion is perpendicular to the view plane.

In order to overcome this problem many authors propose to use multi-camera systems and in particular binocular systems often in stereoscopic configuration. In these systems two or more cameras are used to record the same scene from different points of view. Using specific algorithms, it is possible to recover 3D data about the scene analyzing the various recorded streams. Furthermore this approach helps in reducing the occlusion problem in crowding scenes.

On the other hand, this method requires that the correspondence problem is solved to work properly. This problem refers to locate the match for each pixel of one image with a pixel in the other, and, hence, the name correspondence problem.

Figure 4.1a shows a schematic representation of the correspondence problem. From a geometrical point of view, this problem can be solved using the epipolar geometry.

A. Amato et al., *Semantic Analysis and Understanding of Human Behavior in Video Streaming*, DOI: 10.1007/978-1-4614-5486-1_4,

In literature various authors use this epipolar geometry to solve the correspondence problem. This fact means that they introduce strong constraints on the cameras configuration. For example, a widely applied constraint is that the acquisition system produces stereo images [119, 120]. In this case, the images are taken by two cameras with parallel optic axes and displaced perpendicular to the axes.

Using stereo pairs of images it is possible to assume that: stereo pairs are epipolar and the epipolar lines are horizontally aligned, i.e., the correspondence points in the two images lie along the same scan lines; the objects have continuity in depth; there is a one-to-one mapping of an image element between the two images (uniqueness); and there is an ordering of the matchable points [121].

From a geometric point of view, the corresponding problem can be successfully solved and the methods proposed in literature achieve excellent performance when applied to synthetic images. When these methods are applied to real world images, the main issues to be solved are: noise and illumination changes as a result of which the feature values for the corresponding points in the two images can differ; lack of unique match features in large regions; occlusions, and half occlusions. The wider used methods to solve this problem are: area based [120], feature based [122], Bayesian network [123], neural networks [121, 124], etc.

The stereo-vision approach and, more in general, the multi-camera approach has been applied also to video analysis systems to overcome the occlusion problem and to track people/objects using different cameras [125–128].

In this book, a method to solve the correspondence problem in multi-camera systems based on the merge of two approaches (Self Organizing Map (SOM) and feature based recognition) is proposed. The novelties of this approach are: the proposed method and the ability to work without the assumption of epipolar geometry. Furthermore this method does not require a calibration stage (the initial training of the SOM can not be considered as a calibration stage). This method is not used to fuse two images into one. It is used to find an object into two different images only to handle possible problems of mutual occlusions.

The system must be seen as a stage of the longer processing chain aiming at semantic video analysis (see Fig. 3.1). For this reason, the correspondence problem is not solved for the whole images but only for few relevant points (the barycenters of moving objects).

The remaining part of this chapter is so organized: in Sect. 4.2a brief introduction to the epipolar geometry is presented and in Sect. 4.3 (and in its subsections) the approach to resolve the correspondence problem proposed in this book is shown.

4.2 Epipolar Geometry

Considering Fig. 4.1a [129], let O_L and O_R be the two focal points of the cameras. In real cameras, the image plane is actually behind the focal point, and produces a rotated image. Here, however, the projection problem is simplified by placing a

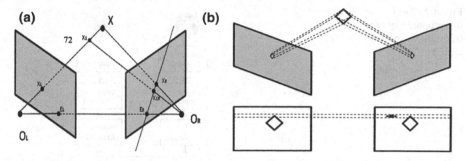

Fig. 4.1 A schematic representation of the correspondence problem (**a**) and the epipolar constraint (**b**)

virtual image plane in front of the focal point of each camera to produce an unrotated image.

Since the two focal points of the cameras are distinct points into the 3D world, each focal point is seen by the other and their projection in the respective image planes are called epipoles or epipolar points (e_L and e_R in Fig. 4.1a). Both epipoles e_L and e_R in their respective image planes and both focal points O_L and O_R lie on a single 3D line.

The left camera sees the line O_L–X as a point because it is directly in line with that camera's focal point. On the other hand, the right camera sees this line as a line in its image plane. The line e_R–x_R in the right camera is called an *epipolar line*. For symmetric reasons, the line O_R–X is seen as a point by the right camera and as epipolar line e_L–x_L by the left camera.

The points O_L, O_R and X define a plane called *epipolar plane*. All the epipolar lines lie on this plane. All epipolar planes and epipolar lines intersect the epipole regardless of where **X** is located.

If the relative translation and rotation of the two cameras is known, the corresponding epipolar geometry leads to two important observations:

- If the projection point x_L is known, then the epipolar line e_R–x_R is known and the point X projects into the right image, on a point x_R which must lie on this particular epipolar line. In other words, for each point observed in one image the same point must be observed in the other image on a known epipolar line. The corresponding image points must satisfy this epipolar constraint. This fact can be used as criterion to verify if two points really correspond to the same 3D point. Epipolar constraints can also be described by the essential matrix between the two cameras. The essential matrix is a 3×3 matrix which relates corresponding points in stereo images assuming that the cameras satisfy the pinhole camera model.
- Using the triangulation method, it is possible to know the 3D coordinate of X knowing the points x_L and x_R.

The epipolar geometry is simplified if the two camera image planes coincide (see Fig. 4.1b). In this case, the search is simplified to one dimension (a horizontal

Fig. 4.2 Block diagram of
the proposed system [117]
(reproduced by permission of
IEEE)

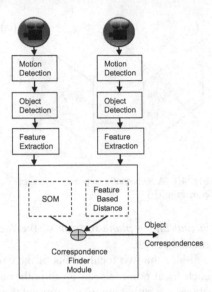

line parallel to the baseline between the cameras O_L–O_R). Furthermore, if the
location of a point in the left image is known, it can be searched for in the right
image by searching left of this location along the line, and vice versa.

4.3 Proposed System

The proposed system uses two cameras (T_1 and T_2) installed in an arbitrary way.
The only constraint is that the scenes recorded by the two cameras must have an
overlapping zone. The greater is the overlapping zone, the greater is the area where
the correspondence problem can be solved.

As shown in Fig. 4.2 [117], the system has a modular architecture. The stream
sampled by each camera follows the chain:

motion detection → object detection → feature extraction → correspondence
finder

4.3.1 Motion and Object Detection Module

The models of the target objects and their motions are considered unknown, so as
to achieve maximum application independence. In this condition, the most widely
adopted approach for moving object detection with fixed camera is based on
background subtraction [130]. The background is estimated using a model
evolving frame by frame. The moving objects are detected by the difference
between the current frame and the background model. A good background model

should be as close as possible to the real background and it should be able to reflect as soon as possible the sudden change in the real background.

According to the taxonomy proposed in [131], the proposed system considers the following objects:

- **Moving visual object** (**MVO**): a set of connected pixels moving at a given speed
- **Background** is the current model of the real background
- **Ghost**: a set of connected pixel detected as "in motion" by the subtraction algorithm but not corresponding to any real moving object.

The proposed system uses these three elements to implement an object oriented motion detection algorithm. It uses the knowledge about the segmented objects to dynamically improve the background model. In order to classify the object after the blob segmentation the following rules are used:

1. <MVO> ← (foreground blob) Λ (large area) Λ (high speed)
2. <GHOST> ← (foreground blob) Λ (large area) $\neg$ (high speed)

4.3.2 Features Extraction Modules

After a MVO is detected, it is described using a Content Based Image Retrieval (CBIR) technique. CBIR is the application of computer vision dealing with the problem of retrieving a set of relevant images from an image database [132–134]. These systems work implementing the following general scheme:

Stimuli → Signatures → Distance

Stimuli are sought as points in some perceptual space [135] while the notion of similarity between two stimuli is one of the fundamental concepts of the cognitive theories of similarity. For the visualization of the underlying ideas, refer to Fig. 4.3 [75].

Consider two different images from the semantic point of view. Let A_p be the semantic (human centric) space. In this space for each image there is a stimulus. On its basis, it is easy for a human being to assess the similarity between two or more images. CBIR systems try to emulate this cognitive chain. Such systems associate a signature (A_s and B_s in Fig. 4.3) to each image defining a signature space. By endowing the signature space with a distance model it is possible to define an artificial similarity space in which it is possible to measure the distance between two or more images (denoted here by A_{a-b} and A_{b-a}). In many distance models (such as the one utilized in this work) symmetry property is assumed to be valid, namely make A_{a-b} equal to A_{b-a}. There could be other constructs such as, e.g., Tversky's "contrast model" [136] in which the symmetry requirement is not used. Indeed, a central assumption of this model is that the similarity between object A and B is a function of the features which are common to A and B ("A and B"), those in A but not in B (symbolized as "A–B") and those in B but not in A

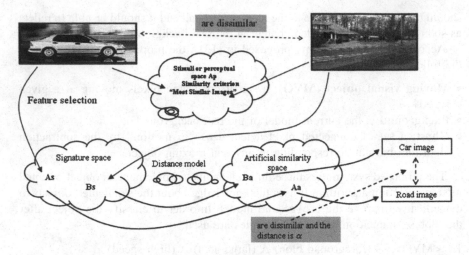

Fig. 4.3 Relationship diagram between images stimuli → signatures → distance (computable similarity) [75] (reproduced by permission of IEEE)

(denoted by "B–A"). Based on this concept and several other assumptions, Tversky postulated the following relationship:

$$S(A,B) = xf(A \text{ and } B) - yf(A - B) - zf(B - A) \qquad (4.1)$$

where S is an interval scale of similarity, f is a function of salience of the various features which have been considered, and x, y and z are weights that underline the relations among the features of the objects in A and B.

Following this scheme (in the form of the chain of associations *stimuli → signatures → distance*), several hypotheses have been investigated. In the purely psychological approach based on multidimensional representation, an image is represented as a point in some highly dimensional space [137]. The location of the point is typically determined with the use of some scaling techniques such as e.g. Multidimensional Scaling (MDS) [138]. The MSD leads to a non-metric space.

The goal is to find a projection space in which the inter-point distance is monotonically related to a human panel response about (di-) similarity. In the purely computational approach, a natural scene is represented by means of a collection of values (*signatures*) explicitly derived from the 2D image containing basic low level features. These could be comparable to such features as retinal-brain sensitivity including shape, colors, and patterns.

In this book, each MVO is characterized by means of two low level visual features (signatures): color histogram and texture. These features were used in many Content Based Image Retrieval (CBIR) systems [75, 139–141].

The color histogram is computed using the Hue, Saturation and Value (HSV) color space (Fig. 4.4). This color space was developed in the late 1970 by computer graphics researchers because they recognized that the geometry of the Red

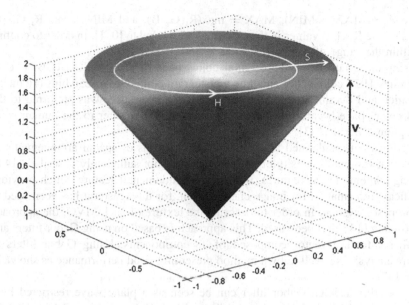

Fig. 4.4 Schematic representation of the HSV color space

Green Blue (RGB) model (that is the widest used color space in all the common electronic color devices) was poorly aligned with the color-making attributes recognized by human vision.

HSV arranges the colors on a cylinder where the *hue* is an angle (0–360) representing the pure color (red, magenta, yellow, etc.). The distance to the centre is the *saturation* going from the pure color (1.0 = fully saturated) to white (0.0 = no saturation). The height within the cylinder represents the *value* or brightness of the color, going from completely bright (1.0) to no brightness (black, 0.0).

The mathematical transformation from RGB to HSV could be computed using the following equations [142]:

$$H = \begin{cases} 60\left(\dfrac{G-B}{\delta}\right) & \Leftrightarrow MAX = R \\[2mm] 60\left(\dfrac{B-R}{\delta}+2\right) & \Leftrightarrow MAX = G \\[2mm] 60\left(\dfrac{R-G}{\delta}+4\right) & \Leftrightarrow MAX = B \\[2mm] notdefined & \Leftrightarrow MAX = 0 \end{cases}$$

$$S = \begin{cases} \dfrac{\delta}{MAX} & \Leftrightarrow MAX \neq 0 \\[2mm] 0 & \Leftrightarrow MAX = 0 \end{cases}$$

$$V = MAX$$

(4.2)

where $\delta = (MAX - MIN)$, $MAX = \max(R, G, B)$, and $MIN = \min(R, G, B)$. Note that the R, G, B values in the equations are scaled to [0, 1]. In order to confine H within the range of [0, 360], $H = H + 360$, if $H < 0$.

Using these equations, the original color space of each MVO (RGB) is converted into HSV color space and then a histogram composed of 256 bins (16 hue, 4 saturation and 4 value levels) is computed. This color space was preferred to the RGB color space because the former is closer than the latter to the human color perception scheme [143].

Textures can be defined as 'homogeneous patterns or spatial arrangements of pixels that regional intensity or color alone does not sufficiently describe' [144]. Among contents based features, texture is a fundamental feature which provides significant information for image classification, for this reason it has been used in the proposed system. In order to describe the texture of each MVO, the approach proposed in [145] has been used. This approach is based on using Gabor filters and defining a feature vector composed of 48 components. Using Gabor filters in texture analysis is a well known method presenting good performance as shown in [146, 147].

A two dimensional Gabor filter can be seen as a plane wave restricted by a Gaussian envelope function. A two dimensional Gabor function g(x,y) can be written as:

$$g(x,y) = \frac{1}{2\pi\sigma_x\sigma_y} e^{-\frac{1}{2}\left(\frac{x^2}{\sigma_x^2} + \frac{y^2}{\sigma_y^2}\right)} e^{i2\pi f_0 x} \tag{4.3}$$

where σ_x and σ_y are the spreads of the Gaussian and f_0 is the spatial frequency of harmonic wave. Gabor functions form a complete but non-orthogonal basis set. Expanding a signal using this basis provides a localized frequency description. Starting from the Gabor function, often called *mother Gabor wavelet*, it is possible to define a self-similar filter dictionary through the appropriate dilatations and rotations of $g(x,y)$. This dictionary is used to decompose the input image into $s \times \theta$ filtered images where s represents the number of scales and θ is the number of orientations. In other words, the input image is analyzed at s different scales to capture different level of details. At each scale, the image is analyzed to evaluate the presence of components at θ different orientations. For each filtered image two features are extracted: mean value and standard deviation. The so obtained feature vector is composed of $s \times \theta \times 2$ components. The experiments reported in this book are based on a feature vector composed of 48 components where $s = 4$ and $\theta = 6$.

Furthermore, for each MVO the bounding box vertex coordinates and the barycenter coordinates are computed.

4.3.3 Correspondence Finder Module

The main task of this module is to define a mapping among the MVOs present in the various frames extracted simultaneously by the two cameras. It works using two different methods to find the matching among MVOs: SOM and the distance among their visual features.

The SOM has been chosen because they have the property of effectively creating spatially organized "internal representation" of various features of input signals and their signatures. The training stage is unsupervised. At each training step, the node/neuron closer (in the Euclidean sense) to the input vector is considered the winner. Its weight vector is updated to move it closer to the input vector in the weight space. All the neighboring nodes/neurons are updated in a weighted way.

The proposed approach is inspired by the work in [121] where the authors propose to use a SOM to obtain a dense disparity map between two images. In this book, this approach is used to define a sort of raw region mapping between the images sampled by the two cameras. In this way, the SOM is used to measure the distance between the barycenter of a MVO in a frame and all the barycenters of the MVOs in the frame taken by the other camera. The time correspondence of two frames taken by the two cameras is assured by the acquisition system that labels in real time the frame sampled by each camera with the timestamp. Let $C_1(x',y')$ be the coordinates of the first MVO barycenter in a frame taken by one camera. Using the SOM, it is possible to map C_1 in the frame taken by the other camera obtaining the coordinates $C_1(x'',y'')$. In this way it is possible to measure the distance between $C_1(x'',y'')$ (and hence the MVO$_1$ represented by C_1) and all the barycenters of the other MVOs in the frame taken by the second camera. The Euclidean distance is used to measure the distance among the various MVOs.

The second method uses the visual features extracted by each MVO to define a mapping among the MVOs in the frames taken by the two cameras. For each MVO present in each couple of frames sampled simultaneously by the two cameras, the extracted features are used to find the correspondence. This module computes the distance among the visual features using a weighted normalized Euclidean distance. This kind of distance is used to consider the similarity contribute of both the features. In the proposed experiments, the weight is equal to 0.5 to give the same relevance to both the features.

The two methods are merged using a weighted distance function (Eq. 4.4). Let X and Y be the sets of MVOs in the frame taken by T_1 and T_2 respectively, let $x \in X$ be a MVO in T_1 and $y \in Y$ a MVO in T_2, then the distance between x and y is computed using the following function:

$$d(x,y) = \alpha d_1(x,y) + (1 - \alpha)[\beta d_2(x,y) + (1 - \beta)d_3(x,y)] \qquad (4.4)$$

where d_1 is the Euclidean distance between the barycenter of x and y after the SOM mapping, d_2 and d_3 are Euclidean distances applied respectively to color feature and texture feature. α and β are the weights used to merge the proposed methods.

4.4 Summary

In this chapter a new method to perform images fusion in multi-camera systems, by identifying the corresponding points in the various images without the assumption of epipolar geometry has been presented.

This method must be seen as a stage of the longer processing chain aiming at semantic video analysis. Since it works at the level of the tracking algorithm reducing the problem of mutual occlusions among MVOs, it can improve the results obtained by the proposed methodology for semantic analysis of video streaming but the latter can work also without the former (the semantic analysis module can work also in system using a single camera).

The proposed method is based on the fusion of two different approaches: SOM and CBIRs.

The SOM is used to create a sort of feature based mapping between some relevant points into the two images. It should be noticed that it works only on the background of the scenes. In this way, giving the coordinate of a point in an image, it is possible to find its coordinates into the other image (with a certain level of approximation).

The CBIRs based module describes the detected moving objects present into the two images using two low level visual features (colors and texture). Using this description, this module finds the correspondence among the moving objects present in the two images.

The system uses both this methods weighting their outputs to find the final list of corresponding objects (and their coordinates) into the two frames.

The ratio behind this approach is to enrich the information in the visual features (those used by the CBIR based module) with geometrical information (the output of the SOM).

Using this method, it is possible to reduce the problem of occlusions in crowding scenes and the sensory gap. Indeed, when the system does not find the correspondence between some MVOs into the two frames it means that an occlusion condition has been detected. These conditions are handled at a higher level of the processing chain by the tracking algorithm.

In literature there are other methods that could be used to perform this task. For example, in the framework of CBIR systems an interesting alternative can be the use of salient points. This kind of technique works on local aspects of the images and it finds a wide application in CBIR systems [148–150]. An interesting point is characterized by two properties: distinctiveness and invariance. This means that a point should be distinguishable from its immediate neighbors and the position as well as the selection of the interesting point should be invariant with respect to the expected geometric distortions [151].

A comparative evaluation between the proposed method and one based on salient points has not been carried out because the book is focused on the high semantic level analysis of video streaming and this module is only functional to the main goal. This approach was introduced to build a solid base for the next processes in the computational chain. It is possible to change this module in order to implement any methods. This fact does not change the methodology used for the semantic analysis of the videos, it can only improve its accuracy.

Chapter 5
Semantic Analysis

This chapter describes the second and most important original contribution of this book namely a methodology to implement systems suitable for high semantic level analysis of video streaming recorded into a narrow domain. This methodology is independent by the method proposed into the previous chapter. Since the latter improves the performance of the object tracking algorithm, the former works with or without the latter. This methodology can work also using single camera systems. The chapter starts with a brief problem overview and then presents the proposed methodology.

5.1 Introduction

As shown in Fig. 3.1, the semantic analysis of human behavior is the last stage of a complex processing chain.

This chapter presents the grammar based methodology proposed in this book. This methodology allows for a hierarchical analysis of the recorded scene. According to the level of details used in scene recording, this methodology can provide from a semantic analysis of the whole scene till a detailed behavior analysis of a single person. From this perspective, this methodology can be seen as a unifying approach to the three classes of methods described in the Chap. 3.

The grammar based approaches, as shown in Chap. 3, allow for human behavior recognition and classification. The ability to define dynamically, for example using some clustering methods, the classes of the observed scenes is not present in other powerful tools used in literature such as the Hidden Markov models (HMM).

The proposed methodology starts from the idea at the base of the scene interpretation systems that try to interpret the scene studying the trajectories of some relevant points of the moving objects (their barycenters). The idea behind this kind

A. Amato et al., *Semantic Analysis and Understanding of Human Behavior in Video Streaming*, DOI: 10.1007/978-1-4614-5486-1_5,
© Springer Science+Business Media New York 2013

of approaches is the mapping between trajectories and behaviors. The ratio can be synthesized into the observation that in order to accomplish a given task one must follow a prefixed series of movements.

In this book, the trajectories are represented by means of string of symbols (the alphabet of the domain specific grammar) each one having a semantic value into the specific domain. The mapping among symbols and the semantic meaning of areas of the scene is done manually at design time. For each domain of application, a grammar is defined in order to specify the recognizable sentences of that domain. In this way it is possible to define a correspondence between the set of the sentences writable with this grammar and the set of allowed actions in the scene.

Since the mapping among portions of scene and symbols/semantic meanings and the grammar are specific for each application, this system belongs to the class of narrow domain systems.

In general, the main drawback of the existing approaches to semantic analysis of the human behavior, even in narrow domains, is inefficiency due to the high computational complexity related to the complex models representing the dynamics of the moving objects and the patterns of the human behaviors. In this perspective this book explores an innovative, original approach to human behavior analysis and understanding by using the syntactical symbolic analysis of video streaming described by means of strings of symbols.

The remaining part of this chapter is so organized: in Sect. 5.2 the key elements of the proposed context switching from trajectories to word is presented, an overview of the proposed methodology is shown in Sect. 5.3. In 5.4 some relevant aspects about grammars and languages are introduced, in Sect. 5.5 the used grammar is shown in details and in 5.6 the aspects related to the time are discussed.

5.2 Switching Domains: From Trajectories to Words

This approach introduces a domain switching for the problem of trajectories analysis. Indeed, by labeling the environment, it is possible to "translate" the geometric data about the trajectories into words. In this way, studying the characteristic of a word means to study the geometric characteristic of a trajectory. So the geometric analysis becomes a linguistic problem.

From this perspective, the problem changes its appearance. The issue of understanding which behaviors (and so which trajectories) are allowed in a given environment become the issue of understanding which words one can write using the symbols (labels) defined for that environment.

This problem can be faced defining a specific grammar for each environment. This approach gives a strong flexibility and reliability to the proposed methodology. Indeed, in this context, defining a grammar means to define the utilizable rules to write the words describing the behaviors. In this way, this methodology inherits one of the most interesting characteristics of the language theory: the possibility of defining infinite set of words (behaviors) starting from a finite set of symbols (the labels used to describe the domain of interest).

This aspect is very important and represents a significant advantage of the grammar based approaches in comparison with other statistic methods (for example the HMM). Indeed, also thinking at a method based on a learning process, it is well known that it is able to recognize all the behaviors that belonged to the training set. Of course, there is the process of generalization, but human behavior analysis is a complex task. Here, this property gives robustness to small changes into the observed behaviors but, for example, it does not give to the system the ability to recognize for example a complex behavior composed of the concatenation of two successive behaviors (also if both these behaviors belonged to the training set).

Defining the grammar for a given domain of interest (namely the environment from which the scenes are recorded), it is possible to define a set of rules allowing to discriminate between words belonging to that grammar (corresponding to the set of allowed behaviors) and words do not (corresponding to forbidden behaviors).

From this point of view, this methodology can be used to implement systems that are able to recognize a large number of behaviors and to raise alarms when a given behavior is not recognized.

Figure 5.1 stresses the concept of mapping among domains showing the successive translations among the three domains under analysis: real world human behavior, trajectory and linguistic.

Figure 5.1a, shows a schematic overview of a real world room. A man has entered from the door (the brown rectangle) and he is walking along the perimeter of the room. He stops his walk into a certain position. This corresponds to the behavior of entering into a room and going to a specific position. This representation shows all the positions occupied by the man during his walk into a single frame. To highlight his actual position, his shape has been drawn darker in the last frame than in the previous frames.

This behavior is projected into the domain of the trajectory as shown in Fig. 5.1b. Here the man is represented by his barycenter (the red points into the figure) and its trajectory is represented by a curve intersecting his barycenter in the successive frames.

This curve in the domain of the trajectory is translated into a word in the linguistic domain. This process is represented in Fig. 5.1c. The floor of the room is virtually divided into twelve areas each one labeled using a letter of the English alphabet. The portion of the curve falling into a given area is coded using the label of that area. In this way, a trajectory is transformed into a word by means of the concatenation of all symbols labeling the areas on which the curve lies.

Following this processing chain, it is possible to obtain a mapping between human behaviors and words.

On the other hand, this methodology allows for an improvement in the semantic level of the human behavior analysis. Indeed, at design time, it is possible to create a mapping between some symbols and some relevant semantic concepts.

For example, it is possible to think that the room represented in Fig. 5.1 is a laboratory of information science and that a printer is installed in the area labeled

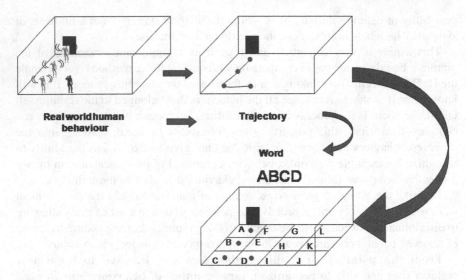

Fig. 5.1 An example of domain conversion. The real world action (**a**) is "translated" into a curve in the domain of the trajectories (**b**). The trajectory is "translated" into a word into the linguistic domain (**c**)

with the letter *"D"*. **In this perspective, this methodology allows for implementing systems exploiting a higher level of semantic analysis of the human behaviors than systems that are only able to classify a behavior as belonging to a known class or not.** Indeed, the word *"ABCD"* that is written by the system in the example of Fig. 5.1, it is not only a *"correct"* word (because it is a word that belong to the language defined on the grammar written at design time) and thus an allowed behavior, but it describes the action of *"a man who enters into the room and goes to the printer"*.

Another aspect to be considered of the proposed methodology is the used model of the real world and in particular of the human behaviors. Indeed, this model represents each behavior as a string of symbols (letters of English alphabet). In this way, the recorded scenes can be represented by means of strings having a high semantic content. As it is well known, the strings are variables easily handled by the modern computers. This approach is not affected by the inefficiency due to the high computational complexity related to the complex models representing the dynamics of the moving objects and the patterns of the human behaviors that are typical of other approaches present in literature.

Furthermore, since this methodology realizes a mapping between the domains of human behaviors and words, storing strings into a database is equivalent to logging human actions. So, it is possible to create databases handling simple variables and using all the powerful research features of the modern database management systems.

From this perspective, the proposed methodology allows for the implementation of advanced system for semantic video indexing.

5.3 Overview of the Proposed Methodology

Figure 5.2 shows a schematic overview of the proposed method for human behavior analysis.

In the bottom left part of the figure, a schematic example of an indoor environment is presented. At design time, the environment is virtually divided into a certain number of areas and each area is labeled with a symbol (in this book, letters of the English alphabet have been used). It is possible to define areas of whatever shapes and dimensions.

It is also possible to define areas of different dimensions among them. The only constraints are:

- There are no overlapping areas
- Each portion of the environment belongs to an area (namely, the partition must completely cover the area under analysis)

This fact allows for a more accurate definition of the areas around some particularly relevant points, namely the areas where it is possible to attribute specific semantic meanings (see the above example of the printer).

The dimension of the areas should be coherent with: the scale of observation of the environment (hence with the resolution of the video streaming) and with the typical speed of the MVOs in the environment under analysis. In other words, the partition should be defined in order to obtain a good resolution in the successive stage of string generation. This is a critical parameter because if the areas are too small in comparison to the speed of the MVOs, it is possible that a given MVO goes from an area to another without passing among all the adjacent areas. In this condition, the parser will not recognize this word and it will consider this one as a forbidden behavior.

The choice of the correct dimension of each area can be straightaway solved in an automatic way, implementing an early learning stage where the system analyzes the mean speed of the MVOs.

Each trajectory should be represented by a string of symbols with at least a symbol for each semantic area that it crosses.

This great flexibility into the partition of the environment and, from a certain point of view, the coarse grain at which this methodology analyzes the trajectories make the system very robust to all the typical problem related to the presence of noise into the input data.

This consideration derives directly from the process at the base of the double context switching from human behavior to trajectory and from trajectory and word described above. Indeed, a human (or whatever portion of interest according to the scale of observation of the problem) is represented analyzing only a point (his barycenter). The position of this point into the room can also be determined with a low level of precision because the useful data are not its coordinates but the label of the area that contains it.

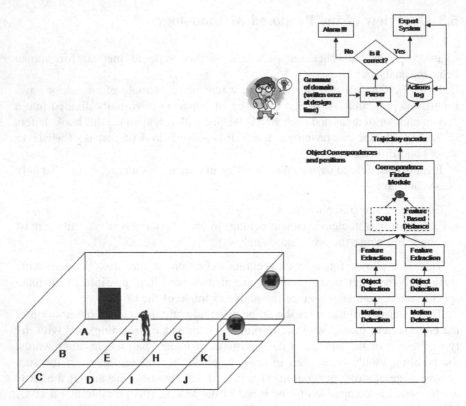

Fig. 5.2 A schematic overview of the proposed methodology

Starting from these considerations, **this methodology does not require techniques to handle the uncertainty due to the noise into input data**.

As shown in Fig. 5.2, this methodology can take advantage of the multi-camera system described in the Chap. 4 (but the methodology is applicable also to single camera systems). Indeed, having a binocular vision, it is possible to:

- improve the precision of the coordinate of the barycenters of moving objects;
- alleviate the problem of partial occlusions in crowded scenes.

The stream sampled by each camera follows the chain:

$$\text{motion detection} \rightarrow \text{object detection} \rightarrow \text{feature extraction}$$
$$\rightarrow \text{correspondence finder}$$

The output of the correspondence finder module consists of the list of object correspondences and their coordinates (Fig. 5.2).

The tracking algorithm uses a string for each detected moving object, hence, the output of the correspondence finder module is used to update these strings (see the module "trajectory encoder" in Fig. 5.2) appending the symbols with which are labeled the relative areas.

The process of strings generation and update is described in the Fig. 5.3. This figure shows two possible events that can occur during a scene recording. In Fig. 5.3a, an example of a man moving inside the same area is shown. In this case, no one symbol is appended to the end of the string used to track his movements. Figure 5.3b shows an example of a man moving from one area to another. In this case, the label of the new area is added to the string ("*D*" in the proposed example).

From a theoretical point of view, it should be noticed that, using this procedure, it is possible to generate any kind of string. On the other hand, the real world phenomenon under analysis (i.e., the motion of a man into a room) has its physical constraints. For example, looking at Fig. 5.3b, for the principle of continuity of motion, when the man is in the area "*D*", he can not go directly into the area "*J*".

He should follow a path through the area "*I*" or a longer path through the other neighborhood areas. Furthermore, it is possible that in a real world case there are other constraints. For example, it is possible that a desk is positioned in the area "*E*". In this case, no one can walk on this area. Other possible constraints can be introduced according to the analyzed scene.

Using the proposed methodology, the respect of these constraints has a straightforward implementation. Indeed, thanks to the double context switching from real world motion to trajectory and from trajectory to string, this methodology allows to face this problem as a linguistic one.

In this context, there is a reliable methodology derived from the language theory to evaluate if a given *string* belongs to a given language (and so it is correct) or not.

5.4 Grammars and Languages

Formal languages are defined with respect to a given alphabet. The alphabet is a finite set of symbols, each of which is called a *letter*. It should be noticed that the terms "letter" does not refer to the "ordinary" letters but it refers to any symbols like numbers, digits, and words. Each finite sequence of letter is defined string or word.

Given an alphabet Σ, the set of all strings over Σ is denoted by Σ^* (where * is the Kleene operator). Notice that no matter what the alphabet is, Σ^* is always infinite. Indeed, even for an alphabet composed of a single letter (for example the letter a), Σ^* contains all the combination of this symbol (a, aa, aaa, $aaa...$).

A formal language over an alphabet Σ is a subset of Σ^*. A language is defined as a subset of Σ^*. It can be, finite or infinite. Since Σ^* is always infinite, given any alphabet Σ, the number of formal languages over Σ is infinite.

In order to specify a language, it is possible to use a generative approach by means of the concept of **grammar**. A grammar could be seen as set of rules which manipulate symbols. There are two kinds of symbols: **terminal** ones, which should be thought of as elements of the target language, and **non-terminal** ones, which are auxiliary symbols that facilitate the specification. The non-terminal symbols can be considered as syntactic categories. Similarly, terminal symbols might correspond to letters of some natural language, or to words.

(a)

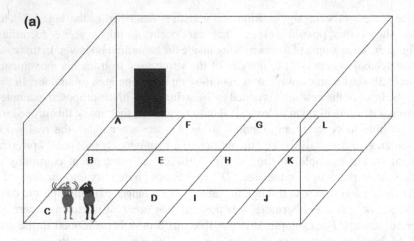

(b)

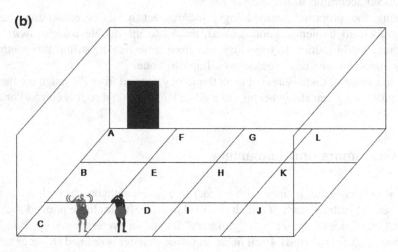

Fig. 5.3 Schematic representation of the process of string generation

Rules are used to express the internal structure of "phrases", which should not necessarily be viewed as natural language phrases. Rather, they induce an internal structure on strings of the language, but this structure can be arbitrary, and should be motivated only by the convenience of expressing the required language. A rule is a non-empty sequence of symbols, a mixture of terminals and non-terminals, with the only requirement that the first element in the sequence be a non-terminal one.

A grammar is a finite set of rules. Formally, a grammar is defined by a four-tuple $G = (V, \Sigma, P, S)$, where V is a finite set of non-terminal symbols, Σ is an alphabet of terminal symbols, P is a set of rules and S is the start symbol, a distinguished member of V. The rules (members of P) are sequences of terminals and non-terminals with a distinguished first element which is a non-terminal.

A well accepted method to represent the rules is the use of expressions like:

S → A

S → AB | a

In these examples of expressions, the following elements are present:

- capital letters of the English alphabet: they represent the non-terminal symbols;
- lower case letter of the English alphabet: they represent the terminal symbols;
- the symbol '→', which means 'produce', represents the relation that exists between various strings of non-terminals and terminals;
- the symbol '|' means 'or'; in the above example, it means that the non-terminal symbol 'S' can produce either two non-terminal symbols 'AB' or the terminal symbol 'a'.

A language L over a grammar G is represented by the symbol L(G) and can be informally defined as the set of all the possible strings that can be generated by G.

Noam Chomsky classified grammars into four types now known as the *Chomsky hierarchy*. The difference between these types is that they have increasingly stricter production rules and can express fewer formal languages.

The Chomsky hierarchy defines the following levels:

- Type-0 grammar (unrestricted grammars) is the set composed of all formal grammars. They are able to generate all the languages that can be recognized by a Turing machine. These languages are also known as the recursively enumerable languages.
- Type-1 grammars (context-sensitive grammars) are able to generate the context-sensitive languages. The rules of these grammar are expressed in the form $\alpha A \beta \to \alpha \beta \gamma$ with A a non-terminal and α, β and γ strings of terminals and non-terminals. The strings γ and β may be empty, but γ must be nonempty. The machine that is able to recognize these languages is the linear bounded automaton (a nondeterministic Turing machine whose tape is bounded by a constant times the length of the input.)
- Type-2 grammars (context-free grammars) generate the context-free languages. These are defined by rules of the form A → γ with A a non-terminal and γ a string of terminals and non-terminals. The machine that can recognize these languages is the non-deterministic pushdown automaton. Context-free languages are the theoretical basis for the syntax of most programming languages.
- Type-3 grammars (regular grammars) generate the regular languages. Such a grammar restricts its rules to a single non-terminal on the left-hand side and a right-hand side consisting of a single terminal, possibly followed (or preceded, but not both in the same grammar) by a single non-terminal. The machine that is able to recognize these languages is the finite state automaton. Additionally, this family of formal languages can be obtained by regular expressions. Regular languages are commonly used to define search patterns and the lexical structure of programming languages (Fig 5.4).

Fig. 5.4 A graphical representation of the Chomsky's hierarchy

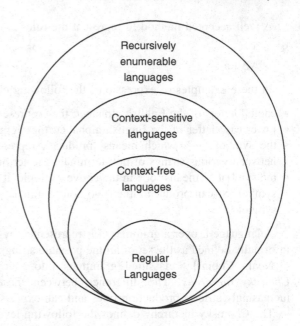

5.5 The Grammar Used in the Proposed Methodology

Using a grammar becomes a cardinal point of the proposed methodology because, as shown above, the grammars can be used to decide if a given string belongs to a given language or not.

Thanks to the proposed double context switch, it is possible to represent behaviors using strings. Hence, it is possible to model the behaviors allowed into a given environment by defining a grammar on the symbols used to label it. This task must be done once at design time. At run time, when the system records and interprets a scene, it translates the observed trajectories into strings and tests if they belong to the defined language or not. If a string does not belong to the defined language, it means that the corresponding behavior does not belong to the set of behaviors considered compatible (or acceptable) in that environment.

The principles used to define a grammar for a given environment can be summarized into the following points:

- Define a virtual partition of the environment under test.
- Attach a label to each element of the partition. These labels will be the non-terminal symbols of the grammar.
- Assume that the entry point of the environment is the start symbol of the grammar.
- For each labeled area, write the production rules that allow to a moving object to go from that area to each allowed adjacent area.

According to the grammar classification proposed by Chomsky, the grammar used in this book belongs to the grammar of type 3, namely it is a regular grammar.

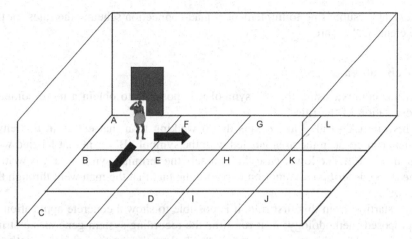

Fig. 5.5 An example of labeled indoor environment with an entering moving object

Indeed, the production rules satisfy the conditions of such kind of grammar (a single non-terminal on the left-hand side and a right-hand side consisting of a single terminal, possibly followed (or preceded, but not both in the same grammar) by a single non-terminal) and overall because all finite languages are regular. The proof of this theorem is carried out using the principle of induction as shown in [152].

The language defined by the proposed grammar can be theoretically composed by a large number of words but this number is finite because the time spent by people in a giving environment is finite.

In the following, an example of definition of such a grammar is proposed.

Figure 5.5 shows a schematic view of an indoor environment. In the right side, two cameras are represented in order to show the compatibility of this methodology with the method to solve the correspondence problem presented in the previous chapter. The environment has been partitioned into twelve areas. Each area has been labeled with a capital letter of the English alphabet.

As said above, formally, a grammar is defined by a four-tuple $G = (V, \Sigma, P, S)$, where V is a finite set of non-terminal symbols, Σ is an alphabet of terminal symbols, P is a set of rules and S is the start symbol, a distinguished member of V.

In this example, the set of non-terminal symbols is:

$V = \{A, B, C, D, E, F, G, H, I, J, K, L\}$

The set of terminal symbols is:

$\Sigma = \{a, b, c, d, e, f, g, h, i, j, k, l\}$

The start symbol is $S = \{A\}$

In order to complete the formal definition of the grammar, the set P, namely the set of production rules, must be defined.

For each area, the production rules to be written are those allowing for the moving object to move from that area to each allowed adjacent areas. Hence, in this example, supposing to implement a quad-connection schema, the rules for the start element "A" are:

S → A
A → aB | aF | a

In this context, using the "|" symbol it is possible to obtain a more compact representation of the rules.

This rule (A → aB | aF) means that a walking man that enters in this environment can go or in the area labeled with the symbol "B" or in that labeled with the symbol "F". The lower case "a", namely the terminal symbol "a", is written in the string describing the motion to record the fact that the man went through the area "A".

Just starting from this first rule, it is possible to show a concrete application of the proposed methodology: if at run-time the recording system generates a string containing the combination of symbols "ae", then the moving object is acting a forbidden behavior because this string does not belong to this grammar.

Figure 5.6 shows another possible configuration: the man has entered into the area labeled with the symbol "B".

Starting from this position, in the real world (with the constraint of the quad-connection schema), the man has three possible chooses of movements: he can go back into the position "A" or he can go forward in position "C" or he can turn left and go in position "E".

The formal rule of the grammar under definition encompassing these three options is:

B → bA | bC | bE | b

One of the areas with the greatest number of possible movements is that labeled with the symbol "E". As shown in Fig. 5.7, starting from the area "E", the man can go in "F" or in "H" or in "D" or in "B".

The formal rule of the grammar under definition encompassing these four options is:

E → eH | eD | eB | eF | e

The complete grammar G = (V, Σ, P, S) for this example can be defined in the following way:

V = {A, B, C, D, E, F, G, H, I, J, K, L}
Σ = {a, b, c, d, e, f, g, h, i, j, k, l}
S = {A}

P is composed of the following rules:

S → A
A → aB | aF | a
B → bA | bC | bE | b
C → cB | cD | c
D → dC | dI | dE | d

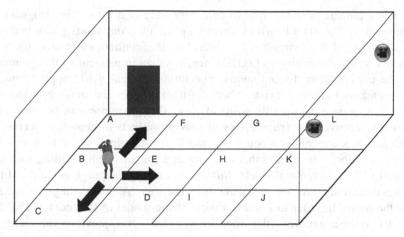

Fig. 5.6 The walking man is in the area "B"

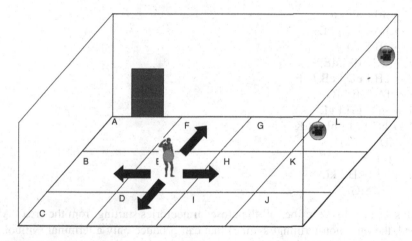

Fig. 5.7 The walking man is in the area "E"

E → eH | eD | eB | eF | e
F → fA | fE | fG | f
G → gF | gH | gL | g
H → hG | hI | hE | hK | h
I → iD | iH | iJ | i
J → jI | jK | j
K → kJ | kH | kL | k
L → lK | lG | l

Analyzing the grammar written for this example, it is possible to make the following considerations:

- On this grammar, it is possible to define the language L(G). This language is composed of the set of strings describing all the continuous paths that are possible into that environment. Hence, all the continuous trajectories will generate strings belonging to L(G). Hence, a system implementing this grammar can be used to find discontinuous trajectories. In real world applications, a discontinuous trajectory exists when the tracker loses the moving object for a fraction of time. **From this point of view, this grammar can be used as a system to recover the trajectories of moving objects in crowding scenes**.
- Each rule produces either a couple (terminal, non-terminal) symbols or a single terminal symbol. This means that this language contains strings ending with any symbol $x \in \Sigma$. In the real world, this means that this language contains all the strings describing trajectories starting from the area "A" and ending everywhere into the room. In order to build a more realistic model of the room in Fig. 5.7 that has only a gateway (the door in area "A"), the previous rules can be rewritten in the following way:

$S \rightarrow A$
$A \rightarrow aB \mid aF \mid a$
$B \rightarrow bA \mid bC \mid bE$
$C \rightarrow cB \mid cD$
$D \rightarrow dC \mid dI \mid dE$
$E \rightarrow eH \mid eD \mid eB \mid eF$
$F \rightarrow fA \mid fE \mid fG$
$G \rightarrow gF \mid gH \mid gL$
$H \rightarrow hG \mid hI \mid hE \mid hK$
$I \rightarrow iD \mid iH \mid iJ$
$J \rightarrow jI \mid jK$
$K \rightarrow kJ \mid kH \mid kL$
$L \rightarrow lK \mid lG$

This set of rules describes all the closed trajectories starting from the area "A". Indeed, the only non-terminal symbol that can produce only a terminal symbol is "A". This is a realistic condition in an indoor environment with a single gateway as that shown in Fig. 5.7.

In Fig. 5.8 a more complex indoor scenario is presented. Also in this scenario the environment has a single gateway, i.e., the door in the area "A". The environment has been partitioned into twelve areas. Each area has been labeled with a capital letter of the English alphabet. In the areas labeled with the symbols "E" and "H" is positioned a desk. In this scenario, a walking man can go everywhere except for the areas "E" and "H" due to the presence of the desk.

Also this scenario can be described with a grammar $G = (V, \Sigma, P, S)$ where:

$V = \{A, B, C, D, E, F, G, H, I, J, K, L\}$
$\Sigma = \{a, b, c, d, e, f, g, h, i, j, k, l\}$
$S = \{A\}$

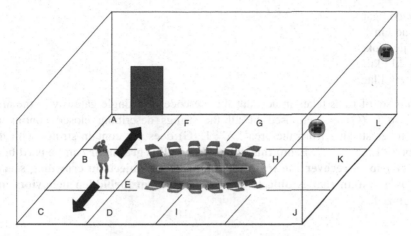

Fig. 5.8 A schematic representation of an indoor environment with a desk in the areas "E" and "H"

The set P must contain the production rules allowing for the definition of a language L(G) that is able to describe all possible trajectories into this environment. The start symbol and the rule for the entering area "A" are the same of the previous example, namely:

S → A
A → aB | aF | a

Figure 5.8 shows another possible configuration: the man has entered into the area labeled with the symbol "B".

This time, starting from this position, in the real world (with the constraint of the quad-connection schema), the man has only two possible choices of movements: he can go back into the position "A" or he can go forward in position "C". He can not turn left and go in position "E" due to the presence of the desk.

The formal rule of the grammar under definition encompassing these three options is:

B → bA | bC

In this way, if at run-time, the recording system generates a string containing the combination of symbols "be", then the moving object is acting a forbidden behavior (he is walking on the desk !!!) because this string does not belong to this grammar. The complete set P is composed of the following rules:

S → A
A → abs | aft | a
B → bad | be
C → cob | cod
D → do | did
F → far | fig

G → go | gal
I → ad | in
J → jig | joke
K → kJ | kill
L → elk | lag

This set of rules takes in account the presence of a single gateway in the area "A", so L (G) is composed of all the strings describing closed continuous trajectories starting from the area "A". L (G) does not contain strings with the symbols "E" and "F". **From this point of view, this grammar can be used both as a system to recover the trajectories of moving objects in crowding scenes and as a system that is able to raise alarms when forbidden behaviors are recognized.**

5.6 The Proposed Methodology and the Time

As shown above, the proposed methodology allows the implementation of systems for high level semantic analysis of human behavior in a given scenario.

Figure 5.9 shows an example of a more complex scenario than that analyzed in the previous examples. This time, the room contains various elements: a printer in area "L", a PC station in "K", a professor's desk in area "J" and a plotter in area "C".

In this scenario, it is possible to say that the string "alfalfa" means "a man has entered into the room, he has taken a print and then he has gone out of the room". In the same way, it is possible to say that the string "afghijihgfa" means "a man has entered into the room, he has gone to the professor desk and then he has come back".

The proposed methodology allows for attributing a high semantic level description to both the events. Nevertheless, a certain level of ambiguity still remains: who was the man that went to the printer? Was he a user that took a print or a technician that repaired the printer? In the same way, who was the man that went to professor's desk? Was he somebody that went to the desk to take a document or the professor that went to his desk to work?

Since this methodology is suitable for systems working in the narrow domain, a possible answer to these questions could result from the analysis of another parameter: **the time**.

Supposing that the room in Fig. 5.9 is a laboratory of a university, it is possible to add more knowledge to the model. For example, in the first example, if somebody goes to the printer to take a print, there is a high probability that this task is executed in few time. Vice versa, if a technician does a work of maintenance of the printer, there is a high probability that this task requires more time than the previous one.

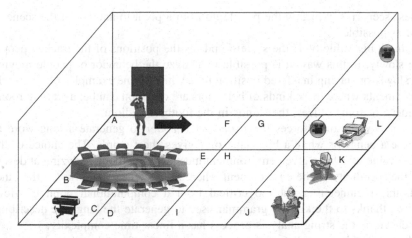

Fig. 5.9 An example of complex indoor scenario

The time plays a fundamental role also in the second scenario. If the man arrives in "J" and stays there for a while, it is very probable that he is the professor. Vice versa, it is probable that he is an assistant taking a document from the professor's desk.

The proposed methodology uses a system for string generation (described in Fig. 5.3) that does not take into account the time of permanence of a moving object in a given area. Indeed, as stated above, in the scenario represented in Fig. 5.3a, where the walking man is moving inside the same area, the system does not produce any symbol. Nevertheless, as further proof of the flexibility of the proposed methodology, in the following **a methodology to handle the time is proposed**.

Thanks to the modularity of the proposed approach, the only module to modify in order to take into account the time is the *trajectory encoder* (see Fig. 5.2). Indeed this module evaluates the coordinates of a given moving object. If these coordinates belong to the same area of the previous recorded point, the system does not generate any symbol. Vice versa, if the coordinates belong to a new area, the system generates the symbol corresponding to its label.

From this perspective, it is possible to say that the *trajectory encoder* has an **event driven** behavior because it generates symbols when a new event (namely a change of area) is recognized.

In order to consider the time, the *trajectory encoder* must have a **time driven** behavior. In this configuration, it generates a symbol ever T seconds. The value of T is a constant for the system and it must be chosen at design time according to the dynamic of the analyzed environment.

A little value of T makes the system more reactive to the rapid changes. In other words, using a small T, it is possible to analyze the behavior of human beings that are moving in a fast way. An example of real world environment where these kinds of behaviors are common can be the corridor of an airport or of a subway station.

In these scenarios, typically the people go from a point to another of the scene as quick as possible.

Using a big value of T, the system updates the positions of the tracked people more slowly. In this way, it is possible to analyze the behavior of people moving very slowly or staying in a fixed position for a while. Some examples of real world environments where these kinds of behaviors are common can be: a waiting room, the queue in some offices, the stands in the football stadium.

A small value of T forces the *trajectory encoder* to generate a long word to describe a behavior while a big value of T gives short words. The choice of the correct value of T for a given environment must be carried out analyzing at design time the specificity of the environment where the system will work. On the other hand, this parameter is not too critical from a computational point of view, because, thanks to the kind of grammar used to generate the language describing the behaviors, the string analysis process has a linear time complexity.

Thanks to this switching of the *trajectory encoder* from event driven to time driven, it is possible to resolve, at certain extent, the examples of ambiguities highlighted in the environment of Fig. 5.9.

Indeed, the behavior of "a man has entered into the room, he has taken a print and then he has gone out of the room" will generate a string similar to: "afglgfa" while the behavior of a technician repairing the printer can be described by: "afglllllllllllllgfa".

In the same way, the assistant that goes and takes a document from the desk of the professor generates the following word: "afghijihgfa" while the professor that goes and works to his desk can generate a string like "afghijjjjjjjjjjjjjjjjjjjjjjjjjjjjjjjjjjjjjjjihgfa".

Hence, introducing the concept of succession of the same symbol into a string and **generating new symbols in time driven modality, it is possible to consider the time using the proposed methodology**.

The grammar used to generate the language describing the allowed behavior in the environment shown in Fig. 5.9 can be the following:

$G = (V, \Sigma, P, S)$ where:
$V = \{A, B, C, D, E, F, G, H, I, J, K, L\}$
$\Sigma = \{a, b, c, d, e, f, g, h, i, j, k, l\}$
$S = \{A\}$

The terminal and the non-terminal symbols sets and the start symbol remain the same of the previous example because the environment has been partitioned and labeled in the same way. The production rule set becomes:

$S \rightarrow A$
$A \rightarrow aF \mid aA \mid a$
$C \rightarrow cD \mid cC$
$D \rightarrow dC \mid dI \mid dD$
$F \rightarrow fA \mid fG \mid fF$
$G \rightarrow gF \mid gL \mid gH \mid gG$
$H \rightarrow hK \mid hG \mid hI \mid hH$

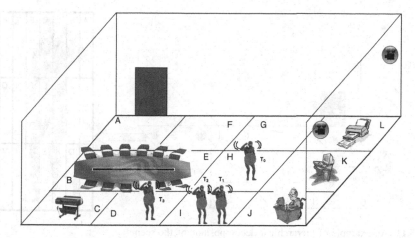

Fig. 5.10 An example of man moving into the room and staying in the same area for $2 \times T$ seconds

I → iD I iJ I iH I iI
J → jI I jK I jJ
K → kJ I kL I kH I kK
L → lK I lG I lL

These rules take into account the fact that the *trajectory encoder* can generate two or more consecutive times the same symbol. Figure 5.10 shows an example of trajectory for a man who goes from the area "H" to "D" staying for $2xT$ in the area "I". The movements are analyzed into the following instants of time:

T_0 the man is in the area "H".
$T_1 = T_0 + T$ the man has gone from "H" to "I"
$T_2 = T_0 + 2*T$ the man has walked between two points of the area "I"
$T_3 = T_0 + 3*T$ the man has gone from the area "I" to that "D"

As the figure shows, at the time T_0 the man is in the area "H". At T_1 the man is arrived in the area "I" starting from "H". This event is recognized and, using the third option of the rule number 7 of the grammar (see the above list), the trajectory encoder writes the symbols "hI" into the string that describes the motion of this man. It should be noticed that "h" is a terminal symbol while "I" is a non terminal one. At T_2 the man is in a position different from that in T_1 but belonging to the same area "I". Also this event is recognized and the trajectory encoder writes the symbols "iI" using the fourth option of the rule 8. Finally, at T_2 he arrives in "D". This time the trajectory encoder writes the symbols "iD" using the first option of the rule 8. At this time the string describing this piece of trajectory is "hiiD" where "h" and "ii" are terminal symbols and "D" is a non terminal one.

Using this grammar, it is possible to write strings describing all the allowed behaviors in this environment. Since forbidden behaviors (such as "going on the desk) are not described by any rules, this grammar can be used to generate alarms

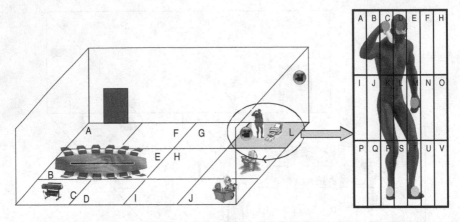

Fig. 5.11 An example of hierarchical decomposition of the scene

when it recognizes a string that does not belong to the language L(G). Furthermore, the strings written by the *trajectory encoder* module are stored into a database that can become the knowledge base of an *expert system* that is able to perform various tasks such as semantic behavior classification and video indexing.

5.7 Hierarchical Scene Analysis

The proposed methodology allows for creating complex systems to perform a hierarchical analysis of the scenes. Indeed, it allows for performing a hierarchical analysis of the recorded scenes defining a different grammar for each level. At the higher level, the behavior of the human beings moving in the scene is analyzed studying their motion parameters (the trajectory that they are following). This process is shown in the left part of Fig. 5.11 and has been described in the previous sections. According to the classification proposed in the related works section, this approach can be considered as belonging to the "scene analysis" class. In this way it is possible to have an analysis of scenario considering the moving objects. At the lowest level, the system can produce a detailed analysis of the action taken by each single human being in the scene.

As shown in Fig. 5.11, some areas of particular semantic interest can be partitioned in a more detailed way. Defining a specific grammar for this area, it is possible to obtain a more detailed semantic analysis of the actions performed in it. At the finest level of detail, this approach can be used in the context of gesture analysis (see the right part of Fig. 5.11). From this perspective this system can be considered as belonging to the class of human recognition systems.

According to the complexity of the task, between these two levels, it is possible to define as many intermediate levels as they are necessary. This hierarchical analysis can exploit the full potentiality of the modern video surveillance systems where there is a fixed camera of scenario and one or more moving cameras that can focus their attention on some areas of interest. In this application, the first level of the proposed hierarchy is applied to the camera of scenario and the second to the moving cameras.

5.8 Summary

In this chapter, the proposed methodology for semantic analysis of video streaming has been presented. This methodology can be seen as a unifying approach encompassing the three main approaches to human behavior analysis existing in literature (scene interpretation, human recognition and action primitive and grammars). Indeed, this methodology allows for a hierarchical analysis of the recorded scene. According to the used level of detail in scene recording, this methodology can provide from a semantic analysis of the whole scene till a detailed behavior analysis of a single person.

This methodology is designed for systems belonging to a narrow domain. The knowledge about the domain is expressed by means of the labeling process. This is a key process enabling the double context-switch from human behaviors to trajectories and from trajectories to strings. In this way, this methodology faces the problem of semantic analysis of human behavior as a linguistic problem.

The language composed of all the words corresponding to allowed human behaviors is obtained using a generative process defining a specific grammar for each domain. This is an interesting aspect of the proposed methodology that overcomes the issues related to the heavy learning process used by other methods.

The trajectory encoder describes all the possible trajectories using the label of the various areas. In this way it is possible to describe complex trajectories such for example zigzag and backward motions. It will be the expert system (Fig. 5.2) that will be able to answer to query about the presence of such kind of trajectories.

The proposed methodology can be used in the implementation of advanced systems for: video surveillance, semantic video indexing, control applications, etc.

Chapter 6
Evaluation of the Proposed Methodology

In this chapter a discussion about the possible applications of this methodology is proposed. Furthermore, the experimental results obtained applying this methodology to a surveillance systems are shown. Also the proposed solution to the correspondence problem has been tested and the obtained results are shown in this chapter.

6.1 Introduction

The proposed methodology is suitable for the design and implementation of systems for semantic analysis of human behavior in streaming video. Such kinds of systems have a great number of possible applications in various fields:

- **Control systems**. In this framework, the proposed methodology allows for the implementation of advanced human–computer interfaces. According to the specific application, the system will focus on the tracking of some relevant body parts (e.g., hands, head, feet). The recorded scene can be partitioned and labeled as shown in Fig. 6.1. Since the trajectory encoder is time driven, it is possible to write a word for the trajectory of each body part without the problem of synchronization. Using a grammar it is possible to define the possible trajectories for each body part. Analyzing the produced strings it is possible to infer the pose of the subject (in the example of Fig. 6.1 "man with raised right hand".
- **Analysis systems**. Applying the same method shown for the control system, it is possible to study also the pose of athletes during their performance. Using a specific grammar, it is possible to write the words corresponding to perfect exercises. In this way, it is possible to implement systems suitable for the processes of training and evaluation of the athletes' performances.
- **Surveillance systems**. As shown in the previous chapter, using the proposed methodology it is possible to design and implement systems for high semantic level analysis of human behaviors. Hence, it is possible to implement video

A. Amato et al., *Semantic Analysis and Understanding of Human Behavior in Video Streaming*, DOI: 10.1007/978-1-4614-5486-1_6,
© Springer Science+Business Media New York 2013

Fig. 6.1 Application to
control systems

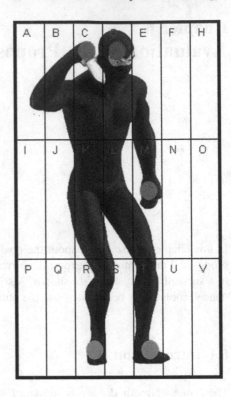

surveillance systems that are able to recognize the behaviors of the monitored
people and raise alarms when forbidden behaviors are recognized.

6.2 Example of Application: Video Surveillance System

To show the effectiveness of the proposed methodology, a demonstrative video
surveillance system has been implemented and applied to a real indoor environment with valuable results. This system has been used also to evaluate the performance of the proposed solution to the correspondence problem in multi-camera
systems.

The system was tested carrying out numerous experiments in a set of indoor
environments of our Faculty. In this book, the tests carried out in a single room of
our Faculty are reported to show how the system works and its potentiality. A
comparative evaluation with other systems present in literature is quite difficult
due to the lack of a common accepted testbed database. The proposed system can
work also in outdoor environments. In this case, only the used motion detection
algorithm should be changed (for example using one modeling the background as a
Gaussian mixture [31]). A screenshot of the monitored room is shown in Fig. 6.2.

Fig. 6.2 A screenshot of the monitored room

The room was virtually divided into a partition as shown in Fig. 6.3. In this example, the red areas (namely the area labeled "C", "E", "I", "K", "J") are forbidden. In the areas "B" and "F" there are two PC stations. The area "G" is in front of the professor's desk. The area "A" is the gateway of the room while areas "D", "H" and "L" are areas where it is possible to walk.

Using these labels, it is possible to associate semantic meaning to each of them and also to their combinations. For example, if the trajectory encoder produces a string with a large number of contiguous "G", there is a high probability that someone is speaking with the professor. In the same way, strings with large numbers of contiguous "F" or "B" mean that somebody is working on the PC in the area "B" of "F".

The grammar used to generate the language describing the allowed behavior in the environment shown in Fig. 6.3 can be the following:

$G = (V, \Sigma, P, S)$ where:
$V = \{A, B, C, D, E, F, G, H, I, J, K, L\}$
$\Sigma = \{a, b, c, d, e, f, g, h, i, j, k, l\}$
$S = \{A\}$

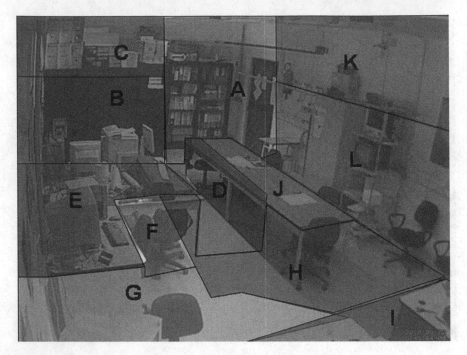

Fig. 6.3 An example of the area partition and mapping

The production rules are:

S → A
A → aB | aD | aL | aA | a
B → bA | bB
D → dA | dH |dD
F → fH | fG | fF
G → gF | gH | gG
H → hD | hF | hG | hL | hH
L → lH | lA | lL

The language L(G) is composed of all the words describing human behaviors considered "normal" at design time. These rules allow behaviors like: walking in the room with whatever trajectory, going to some working stations and staying there for a while and do on.

By the other hands, they do not allow other behavior such as: going on the desks, or climbing on walls. Particular attention requires the area "C". This area comprises a set of PC positioned on a cabinet. These PCs belong to a cluster of workstation. Typically these PCs are managed by remote stations. The only rare operations of ordinary administration can be: power on, insert a DVD, etc.

To avoid that the system raises alarms during these operations, the area "C" was sized in a specific manner. In particular, its size was defined in such a way that

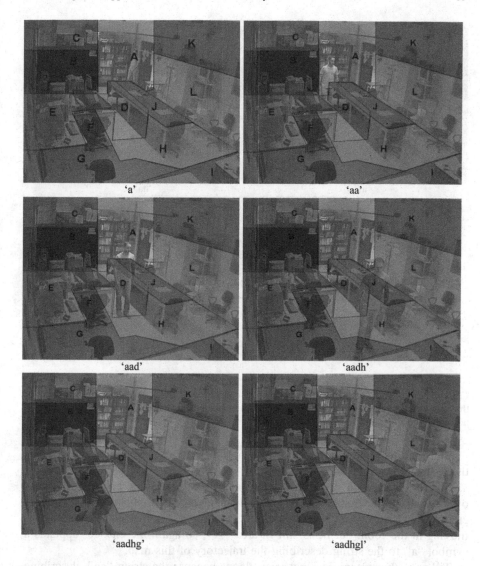

Fig. 6.4 An example of output of the trajectory encoder. For each analysed frame, the label of the area containing the barycenter of the man is appended to the string. All these strings are recognized by the grammar G and so no alarms are raised

during the normal operations, only the user's arms enter in this area. In this way, the barycenter of the user still remains in the area "B" without alarms.

Figure 6.4 shows an example of the output of the trajectory encoder. In this figure, six frames of a video of a walking man are shown. In this sequence, the man enters the door (area "A"), walks into the room (areas "DH") and arrives to the area "G". Then he comes back. Under each frame the output of the trajectory encoder module is shown.

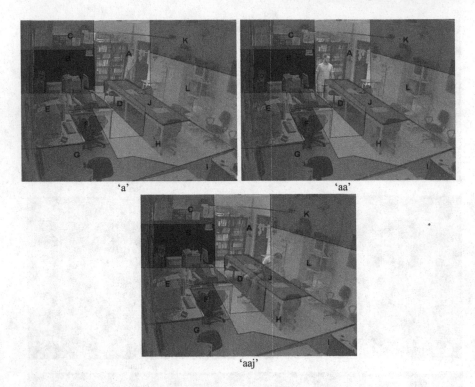

Fig. 6.5 An example of output of the trajectory encoder. For each analysed frame, the label of the area containing the barycenter of the man is appended to the string. Some of these strings do not belong to L(G) and so alarms are raised

Since in this sequence the trajectory encoder writes a word belonging to L(G), the system does not raise alarms.

Figure 6.5 shows a situation where a man has a forbidden behavior (he goes over a desk). In the first frame, he enters in the area "A", so the trajectory encoder creates a void string and appends the first symbol "a". In the second frame, he is moving in the room but he is still in area "A", so again the encoder appends a symbol "a" to the string describing the trajectory of this man.

Till now, the system does not raise alarms because the string "aa", describing the trajectory of the man, belongs to the language L(G). Indeed, it can be produced by applying two consecutive times the production rule number 2.

In the third frame, the man jumps over the desk and his barycenter is in the area "J". This time the trajectory encoder appends the symbol "j" to the string. Now the string becomes "aaj". This string does not belong to the language L(G) because there is no combination of production rules allowing for writing it.

6.3 Example of Application: System for Human Behavior Classification

As it is shown in the previous chapters, systems for human behavior analysis in video streaming typically use a set of algorithms to obtain a "synthetic" pattern representing the recorded scene.

For example, the proposed methodology applies a set of algorithms to obtain a word for each human into a recorded scene representing its behavior.

In the literature there are many advanced technologies for pattern recognition and classification such as neural network and clustering algorithms [153, 154]. Some examples about the application of these technologies to video analysis can be found in [155, 156].

In this chapter the authors show how it is possible to apply a clustering method to the words produced by the proposed methodology to classify human behaviors in a recorded scene.

The clustering technique considered here is the K-medoid.

K-medoid is a partitive clustering algorithm. As the well known k-means algorithm, the target of the k-medoid algorithm is to minimize the distance between all the points of a given cluster and the point designated to be its center. For both these algorithm the number of desired clusters is an input parameter. The main difference between k-means and k-medoid is the method used to compute the coordinates of the center of each cluster. Indeed, k-medoid uses as center a point belonging to the dataset while the k-means uses a virtual point given by the barycenter of the dataset points belonging to a given cluster.

The algorithm works as follows:

a. Randomly select k objects that will serve as the medoids.
b. Associate each data point with its most similar medoid using a distance measure and calculate the cost.
c. Randomly select a new set k objects that will serve as the medoids and save a copy of the original set.
d. Use the new set of medoids to recalculate the cost.
e. If the new cost is greater than the old cost then stop the algorithm.
f. Repeat steps (b) through (e) until there is no change in the medoids.

The cost for the current clustering configuration is calculated using the following equation:

$$C(M,X) = \sum_{i=1}^{n} \min_{j=1}^{k}(d(m_j.x_i))$$

where M is the set of medoids, X is the data set, n is the number of patterns, k is the number of clusters, m_j is the jth medoid, x_i is the ith pattern, and d is a distance function.

Fig. 6.6 A view of the scene
and image data from which
the detected targets are found
(originally published in [157]
and posted in [158];
reproduced by permission of
the authors)

The distance function can be any distance metric, in the experiment presented
in this chapter, the Levenshtein distance has been used. This is a metric for
measuring the amount of difference between two sequences. The Levenshtein
distance between two strings is defined as the minimum number of edits needed to
transform one string into the other, with the allowable edit operations being
insertion, deletion, or substitution of a single character.

The cost function basically calculates the total cost across the entire data set.
The min function is meant to find the medoid that a given pattern is closest to. This
is done by calculating the distance from every medoid to a given pattern and then
adding the smallest distance to the total cost.

It becomes apparent that this clustering process is completed in a fully unsupervised mode; no supervision is offered and the objective function is somewhat
reflective of the geometry of the data so that the minimization of Q leads to an
"acceptable" structure.

The proposed system and the k-medoid algorithm were tested using a publically
available video database: the "Edinburgh Informatics Forum Pedestrian Database"
[157]. This database is composed of a set of detected targets of people walking
through the Informatics Forum, the main building of the School of Informatics at
the University of Edinburgh. The data were sampled for several months and there
are about 1,000 observed trajectories each working day. By July 4, 2010, there
were 27+ million target detections, of which an estimated 7.9 million were real
targets, resulting in 92,000+ observed trajectories. From a functional point of
view, this database can be seen as the output of a video surveillance system with a
fixed camera.

Figure 6.6 (originally published in [157] and posted in [158]) shows a view of
the scene and image data from which the detected targets are found. The main
entry/exit points are marked with arrows. They are placed at the bottom left (front
door), top left (cafe), top center (stairs), top right (elevator and night exit), bottom
right (labs). In the database there are also some false detections due to noise,
shadows, reflections, etc. Normally, only about 30 % of the captured frames

Fig. 6.7 This figure shows
the partition used to label the
scene under analysis. This
figure has been derived by
overimposing the partitioning
and labeling to Fig. 6.6
(originally published in [157]
and posted in [158];
reproduced by permission of
the authors)

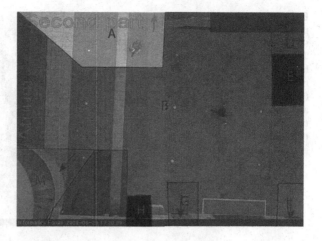

contain a target and normally there are only a few targets in each frame (1 target in
46 % of active frames, 2:25 %, 3:14 %, 4:8 %, 5:4 %, 6 14:3 % of time). The
videos are recorded by a fixed camera overhead approximately 23 m above the
floor. The distance between the 9 white dots on the floor is 297 cm vertically and
485 cm horizontally. The images are 640 × 480, where each pixel (horizontally
and vertically) corresponds to 24.7 mm on the ground.

The database does not contain the raw image data but a set of pre-computed
files describing the trajectories of the detected moving objects. In the database
there is a file for each monitoring day.

In order to test the proposed system, we used the trajectories that have been
detected on 24 August and reported in the video database the "Edinburgh Informatics Forum Pedestrian Database" [157]. On this day, 664 moving objects
(people) have been detected and their trajectories are stored in a single file [159].

On these data, the proposed system has been used to classify the detected
behaviors.

The scene has been partitioned and labeled as shown in Fig. 6.7 (this figure has
been derived by overimposing the partitioning and labeling to Fig. 6.6, which was
originally published in [157] and is posted in [158]). It is possible to notice that the
scene has been partitioned using areas of different sizes. Each area has a homogeneous semantic meaning, for example, the area labeled with the letter "B" is a
transit area while the area "C" represents the gateway to the lifts. Each recorded
trajectory has been translated into a word using the trajectories encoder. In this
framework, for example, when the trajectories encoder produces a string like
"NBBBBC", the expert system infers that a person is walking from the atrium
area to the lifts.

In order to classify all the observed trajectories, a clustering algorithm has been
applied on the dataset composed of all the words encoded by the trajectories
encoder.

Clustering is a well-known technique used to discover inherent structure inside
a set of objects. Clustering algorithms attempt to organize unlabeled pattern

Fig. 6.8 This figure shows a plot of all the 664 trajectories stored into the used dataset. This figure has been derived by overimposing the trajectories to Fig. 6.6 (originally published in [157] and posted in [158]; reproduced by permission of the authors)

vectors into clusters or "natural groups" so that points within a cluster are more similar to each other than to points belonging to different clusters.

For each cluster, the centroid is computed and then it is used as "templates" to represent the entire cluster.

Figure 6.8 shows a plot of all the detected trajectories stored into the dataset under analysis (this figure has been derived by overimposing the trajectories to Fig. 6.6, which was originally published in [157] and is posted in [158]). These trajectories represent all the behaviors detected in a day of monitoring.

As said before, in order to find the most representative behaviors the k-medoid algorithm has been applied to this dataset many times changing the number of clusters. Figures 6.9, 6.10 and 6.11 show the results obtained respectively using 8, 12 and 20 clusters (these figures have been derived by overimposing the obtained results to Fig. 6.6, which was originally published in [157] and is posted in [158]).

These figures highlight the ability of the proposed method to represent in an effective way many different human behaviors. In particular, Fig. 6.11 shows that the proposed system is able to describe all the observed behaviors using only 20 words.

These experiments highlight the feasibility of using the proposed system as a video retrieval system working at high semantic level. In particular, it is suitable for all the videos recorded by the modern video surveillance systems.

6.4 Test of the Proposed Solution to the Correspondence Problem

Some experiments have been carried out to evaluate the effectiveness of the proposed solution to the correspondence problem in multi-camera systems. They have been carried out in the same room of the previous ones using an additional camera as shown in the schema in Fig. 6.12 [117].

Fig. 6.9 A plot of the most frequent trajectories detected using the k-medoid algorithm to obtain 8 clusters. This figure has been derived by overimposing the trajectories to Fig. 6.6 (originally published in [157] and posted in [158]; reproduced by permission of the authors)

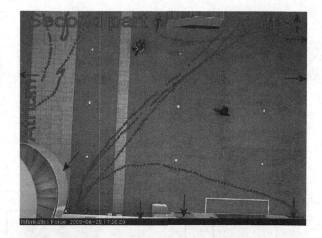

Fig. 6.10 A plot of the most frequent trajectories detected using the k-medoid algorithm to obtain 12 clusters. This figure has been derived by overimposing the trajectories to Fig. 6.6 (originally published in [157] and posted in [158]; reproduced by permission of the authors)

Fig. 6.11 A plot of the most frequent trajectories detected using the k-medoid algorithm to obtain 20 clusters. This figure has been derived by overimposing the trajectories to Fig. 6.6 (originally published in [157] and posted in [158]; reproduced by permission of the authors)

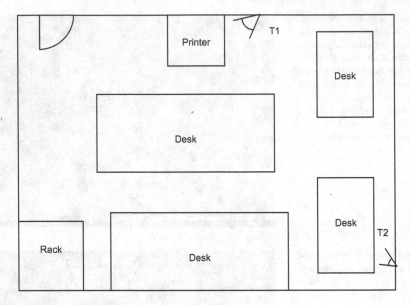

Fig. 6.12 A schematic view of the experiment setup. T_1 and T_2 are the two cameras (reproduced by permission of IEEE)

T_1 and T_2 are the two used cameras. They are installed at a distance of about three meters from the ground plane. In these experiments two Axis 210 network cameras were used. These cameras are able to sample up to 30 frames per second but in these experiments only 15 frames per second were used since a higher frame rate does not introduce more details in the correspondence problem process [117]. Indeed, using more than 15 frames per second the differences between two successive frames sampled by the same camera are negligible.

The SOM is trained using various manually selected relevant points of objects present in the frames sampled by both the cameras. The system was developed using the Matlab® environment. The proposed results are obtained using a SOM with 300 nodes.

In all the experiments both α and β are set to 0.5. In this way both color and texture features and SOM and feature based method are considered with the same relevance. An in-depth research of optimal values for α and β will be matter of future works.

In order to test the system, various sequences were sampled where one or more people are moving in the room. Figure 6.13 [117] shows an example of the obtained results. In the first column there are the frames as they are sampled by the cameras. The recorded scenes are quite complex because both cameras see partial occlusions. Indeed, there is a desk occluding the low part of the walking people. Furthermore there are various "dynamic" occlusions namely occlusions due to the overlap of walking people (this kind of occlusions is typical of crowded scenes). In particular, the first column of Fig. 6.13 shows a frame where two people are walking without "dynamic" occlusions.

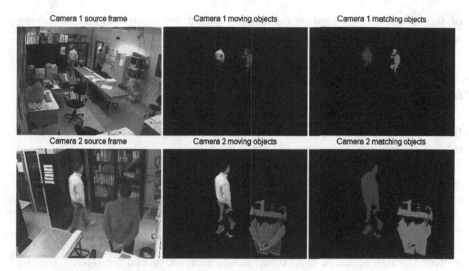

Fig. 6.13 An example of the obtained results [117]. Starting from the left column: source frames, object detection algorithm output, found object correspondences. The corresponding moving objects into the two frames are coloured using the same colour. (reproduced by permission of IEEE)

Table 6.1 Results obtained analysing ten different videos

Number of people	1	2	3
Recall (%)	94	72	77
% false match	4	24	28

The second column shows the output of the proposed object detection algorithm applied to both the cameras.

The third column shows the results obtained by the proposed solution to the correspondence problem applied to these frames. The corresponding moving objects into the two frames are colored using the same color.

Table 6.1 shows some statistics about the mean results obtained by analyzing ten videos where various people are walking into the room. This table shows the obtained recall and the percentage of detected false matching for videos where there were respectively one person, two and three people walking.

The obtained results highlight the effects of occlusion on the proposed system. Indeed, when there is a person walking in the room, the recall is 94 % and the false matches are 4 %. These values are due to the static partial occlusions due to the presence of the desk in the scene. When there are two and three people walking in the room, dynamic occlusions have a clear effect on the performance of the proposed system. Indeed the recall decreases to 72 % for two people and 77 % for three people while the percentage of false matching increases to 24 and 28 % for two and three people walking respectively. These results highlight the robustness of the system to this kind of occlusions. Indeed the recall and false matching remain almost constant in the experiments with two and three people walking.

6.5 Summary

In this chapter possible applications of this methodology have been discussed and related experiments have been reported.

The proposed methodology has a great flexibility. It can be used to describe the actions at various levels of detail. In this way it is possible to implement specific applications in the field of: control, analysis and surveillance systems.

For example, in the proposed test application, the methodology has been applied to implement a surveillance system. It can describe the actions of a human being specifying where he went and how long he was in each position. It should be noticed the high semantic level of the action analysis, indeed the system consider positions as "semantic places". So, considering Fig. 6.3, when the system recognizes that a human being stays for a given period of time in the position "G", it is possible to say that automatically that "a human being stays for a given period in front of professor desk".

This level of details is more than sufficient for the most parts of the video surveillance applications but thanks to the hierarchical approach proposed in this methodology, it is possible to implement a further level of detail where the actions performed in some relevant areas are described. For example, focusing the attention on the area "G" of Fig. 6.3 (the area in front of the professor's desk), it is possible to describe the gesture of the people in that area applying the same methodology. In this way it is possible to implement hierarchical systems having a different level of detail for each level of the hierarchy.

In this chapter has been reported also the results of some experiments carried out to evaluate the performance of the proposed solution to the correspondence problem.

It is difficult to compare the obtained performance with other works in literature. Indeed, in literature there are two main classes of works dealing with the correspondence problem:

1. Works aiming at solving the problem for all the points of the images. These works try to obtain a dense disparity map and they evaluate the performance analyzing the percentage of correctly mapped pixels.
2. Works using the multi-camera vision in video analysis applications (i.e. video surveillance systems). These works do not give too emphasis to the correspondence problem in the performance evaluation sections.

Starting from these considerations, in Table 6.1 the obtained results are presented in terms of recall and percentage of false matching because these parameters can give to the reader an objective idea of the system performance.

Chapter 7
Conclusions

7.1 Concluding Remarks

In this book an innovative methodology to implement systems for high semantic
level analysis in the narrow domain has been presented.

The methodology proposes a double context switch. The first one is from
human motion to barycenter trajectory and is a well known and accepted method
in literature. The second one is an original contribute of this book and is from
trajectory to word. It is based on the domain of application of this methodology,
namely the narrow domain. The external knowledge is introduced into the system
by labeling with a set of symbols the various areas in which the scene is partitioned. The *trajectory encoder* produces a word for each trajectory. The portion of
the trajectory falling into a given area is coded using the label of that area. In this
way, a trajectory is transformed into a word by means of the concatenation of all
symbols labeling the areas on which the curve lies. Furthermore, since the *trajectory encoder* has a **time driven** behavior, this methodology is able to handle the
issues related to the different execution times of the actions.

Since in the narrow domain it is possible to attrib a semantic value at each area
and thus at each symbol, using this methodology it is possible to achieve a high
semantic level description of the recorded scene.

This methodology uses a robust approach to the problem of strings/words
recognition. After the environment has been labeled, a grammar on the set of
symbols used to label the scene is defined. The production rules set of this
grammar contains the rules to describe all the allowed behaviors in a given scenario. Using this grammar it is possible to define a language composed of the set of
recognizable words (and thus the allowed behaviors).

This methodology allows for implementing hierarchical analysis of the scenes
defining a different grammar for each level. At the higher level, the behavior of the
human beings moving in the scene is analyzed studying their motion parameters
(the trajectory that they are following). In this way it is possible to have an analysis

A. Amato et al., *Semantic Analysis and Understanding of Human Behavior
in Video Streaming*, DOI: 10.1007/978-1-4614-5486-1_7,
© Springer Science+Business Media New York 2013

of scenario considering the moving objects and their interactions. At the lowest level, the system can produce a detailed analysis of the action taken by each single human being in the scene. According to the complexity of the task, between these two levels, it is possible to define as many intermediate levels as they are necessary. This hierarchical analysis can exploit the full potentiality of the modern video surveillance systems where there is a fixed camera of scenario and one or more moving cameras that can focus their attention on some areas of interest. In this application, the first level of the proposed hierarchy is applied to the camera of scenario and the second to the moving cameras.

From this point of view, this methodology can be seen as a unifying approach encompassing the three main approaches to human behavior analysis existing in literature (scene interpretation, human recognition and action primitive and grammars).

Another element of innovation of this methodology is the method used for human behavior description and recognition. Indeed, this methodology proposes a generative approach to human behavior recognition. Defining a specific grammar G for a given domain, the system uses its rules to describe a human behavior writing a word. The system is able to recognize all the behaviors that can be described using a word belonging to the language defined on the grammar G. This is a strong improvement in comparison to many works in literature that are able to recognize only a finite set of actions learnt in a training stage.

This book gives also an original contribute to two relevant issues in this research field: sensory gap and partial occlusions proposing a novel solution to the correspondence problem in multi camera systems. This solution is based on the fusion of two approaches: SOM and CBIRs. The SOM is used to create a sort of feature based mapping between some relevant points into the two images while the CBIRs based module describes the detected moving objects present into the two images using two low level visual features (colors and texture). Using this description, this module finds the correspondence among the moving objects present in the two images.

7.2 Future Developments

The proposed methodology allows for a hierarchical analysis of the recorded scene. According to the abstraction level of details used in scene recording, this methodology can provide from a semantic analysis of the whole scene till a detailed behavior analysis of a single person. This architecture has great potentialities but much work is to be done in the definition of the various levels.

In particular, in future works the aspects related to the interactions among human beings can be further analyzed. Since the *trajectory encoder* is time driven, it is possible to maintain a good level of synchronization among the strings describing the behaviors of the various people in the scene. This fact can be the basis for the design of grammars on which to define languages describing various interactions among human beings.

Another aspect to be further investigated is the use of this methodology to implement systems for high semantic level video indexing. The strings produced by the *trajectory encoder* are stored into a database (see Fig. 5.2) called *action log*. Searching for a given string into this database means searching for a given behavior. From this point of view, it is possible to apply techniques of clustering of words on this database to produce a more in depth comprehension of the observed behaviors. This database contains data characterized by a high semantic value, but it requires an advanced human interface that should be able to exploit all the system potentiality.

A limit of the systems implementing the proposed methodology is the fact that they are view dependent. Indeed, the partitioning and labeling of the scene is referred to the camera view. In future works, a solution to this problem can be searched in the framework of the computer vision field and in particular of the CBIR systems.

References

1. Lymberopoulos, D., Teixeira, T., Savvides, A.: Macroscopic human behavior interpretation using distributed imager and other sensors. Proceedings of the IEEE **96**(10), 1657–1677 (2008)
2. Gamassi, M., Piuri, V., Sana, D., Scotti, F., Scotti, O.: Scalable distributed biometric systems—advanced techniques for security and safety. IEEE Instrum Meas Mag **9**(2), 21–28 (2006)
3. Gamassi, M., Lazzaroni, M., Misino, M., Piuri, V., Sana, D., Scotti, F.: Quality assessment of biometric systems: a comprehensive perspective based on accuracy and performance measurement. IEEE Trans Instrum Meas **54**(4), 1489–1496 (2005)
4. Gamassi, M., Lazzaroni, M., Misino, M., Piuri, V., Sana, D., Scotti, F.: Accuracy and performance of biometric systems. In: Proceedings of the 2004 IEEE Instrumentation and Measurement Technology conference IMTC 2004, pp. 510–515, Como, Italy, May 2004
5. Gamassi, M., Piuri, V., Sana, D., Scotti F.: A high-level optimum design methodology for multimodal biometric systems. In: Proceedings of the 2004 IEEE International Conference on Computational Intelligence for Homeland Securit and Personal Safety CIHSPS 2004, pp. 41–45, Como, Italy, July 2004
6. Gamassi, M., Piuri, V., Sana, D., Scotti, O., Scotti, F.: A multi-modal multi-paradigm agent-based approach to design scalable distributed biometric systems. In: Proceedings of the 2005 IEEE International Conference on Computational Intelligence for Homeland Security and Personal Safety CIHSPS 2005, pp. 65–70, Orlando, FL, USA, April 2005
7. Cimato, S., Gamassi, M., Piuri, V., Sana, D., Sassi, R., Scotti, F.: Personal identification and verification using multimodal biometric data. In: Proceedings of the 2006 IEEE International Conference on Computational Intelligence for Homeland Security and Personal Safety CIHSPS 2006, pp. 41–45, Alexandria, VA, USA, Oct 2006
8. Cimato, S., Gamassi, M., Piuri, V., Sassi, R., Cimato, S., Scotti, F.: A biometric verification system addressing privacy concerns. In: Proceedings of the 2007 IEEE International Conference on Computational Intelligence and Security, pp. 594–598, Harbin, Heilongjang, China, Dec 2007
9. Cimato, S., Gamassi, M., Piuri, V., Sassi, R., Scotti, F.: Privacy-aware biometrics: design and implementation of a multimodal verification system. In: Proceedings of the 24th Annual Computer Security Applications Conference ACSAC 2008, pp. 130–139, Anaheim, CA, USA, Dec 2008

A. Amato et al., *Semantic Analysis and Understanding of Human Behavior in Video Streaming*, DOI: 10.1007/978-1-4614-5486-1, © Springer Science+Business Media New York 2013

10. Barni, M., Bianchi, T., Catalano, D., Di Raimondo, M., Donida Labati, R., Failla, P., Fiore, D., Lazzaretti, R., Piuri, V., Scotti, F., Piva, A.: Privacy-preserving fingercode authentication. In: Proceedings of the 12th ACM Multimedia and Security Workshop, pp. 231–240, New York, NY, USA, Sept 2010

11. Cimato, S., Gamassi, M., Piuri, V., Sassi, R., Scotti, F.: A multi-biometric verification system for the privacy protection of iris templates. In: Proceedings of the 2008 IEEE International Workshop on Computational Intelligence in Security for Information Systems CISIS 2008, pp. 227–234, Genova, Italy, Oct 2008

12. Barni, M., Bianchi, T., Catalano, D., Di Raimondo, M., Donida Labati, R., Failla, P., Fiore, D., Lazzeretti, R., Piuri, V., Scotti, F., Piva, A.: A privacy-compliant fingerprint recognition system based on homomorphic encryption and fingercode templates. In: Proceedings of the IEEE Fourth International Conference on Biometrics: Theory, Applications and Systems BTAS 2010, pp. 1–7, Crystal City, VA, USA, Sept 2010

13. Ko, T.: A survey on behavior analysis in video surveillance for homeland security applications. In: Proceedings of the 37th IEEE Applied Imagery Pattern Recognition Workshop AIPR 2008, pp. 1–8, Oct 2008

14. Heckenberg, D.: Performance evaluation of vision-based high DOF human movement tracking: a survey and human computer interaction perspective," In: Proceedings of the 2006 IEEE Conference on Computer Vision and Pattern Recognition CVPR 2006, p. 156, New York, USA, June 2006

15. Saito, H., Inamoto, N., Iwase, S.: Sports scene analysis and visualization from multiple-view video. In: Proceedings of the 2004 IEEE International Conference on Multimedia and Expo ICME 2004, pp. 1395–1398, Taipei, Taiwan, June 2004

16. Mizuno, H., Nagai, H., Sasaki, K., Hosaka, H., Sugimoto, C., Khalil, K., Tatsuta, S.: Wearable sensor system for human behavior recognition (first report: basic architecture and behavior prediction method). In: Proceedings of the 2007 International Conference on Solid-State Sensors, Actuators and Microsystems Conference TRANSDUCERS 2007, pp. 435–438, Lyon, France, June 2007

17. Isoda, Y., Kurakake, S., Imai, K: Ubiquitous sensor-based human behavior recognition using the spatio-temporal representation of user states. Int. J. Wirel. Mobile Comput. 3(1/2), 46–55 (2008)

18. Smeulders, A.W.M., Worring, M., Santini, S., Gupta, A., Jain, R.: Content-based image retrieval at the end of the early years. IEEE Trans. Pattern Anal. Mach. Intell. 22(12), 1349–1380 (2000)

19. Santini, S., Jain, R.: Beyond query by example. In: Proceedings of the 1998 Proceedings of the IEEE Second Workshop on Multimedia Signal Processing, pp. 3–8, Los Angeles, CA, USA, Dec 1998

20. Di Lecce, V., Amato, A., Piuri, V.: Data fusion for user presence identification. In: Proceedings of the 2009 IEEE International Conference on Computational Intelligence for Measurement Systems and Applications CIMSA 2009, pp. 242–246, Hong Kong, China, May 2009

21. Di Lecce, V., Calabrese, M., Piuri, V.: An ontology-based approach to human telepresence. In: Proceedings of the 2009 IEEE International Conference on Computational Intelligence for Measurement Systems and Applications CIMSA 2009, pp. 56–61, Hong Kong, China, May 2009

22. Piuri, V., Scotti, F.: Fingerprint biometrics via low-cost sensors and webcams. In: Proceedings of the 2008 IEEE International Conference on Biometrics: Theory, Applications and Systems BTAS 2008, pp. 1–6, Crystal City, VA, USA, Sept–Oct 2008

23. Philipose, M., Fishkin, K., Patterson, D., Perkowitz, M., Hahnel, D., Fox, D., Kautz, H.: Inferring activities from interactions with objects. IEEE Pervasive Comput. Mag. 3(4), 50–57 (2004)

24. Sugimoto, C., Tsuji, M., Lopez, G., Hosaka, H., Sasaki, K., Hirota, T., Tatsuta, S.: Development of a behavior recognition system using wireless wearable information devices. In: Proceedings of the 1st IEEE International Symposium on Wireless Pervasive Computing ISWPC 2006, pp. 1–5, Phuket, Thailand, Jan 2006

25. Sato, T., Otani, S., Itoh, S., Harada, T., Mori, T.: Human behavior logging support system utilizing fused pose/position sensor and behavior target sensor information. In: Proceedings of 2003 IEEE/ASME International Conference on Multisensor Fusion and Integration for Intelligent Systems MFI 2003, pp. 305–310, Tokyo, Japan, July–Aug 2003

26. Bao, L., Intille, S.S.: Activity recognition from user-annotated acceleration data. In: Proceedings of the 2nd International Conference on Pervasive Computing PERVASIVE 2004, pp. 1–17, Linz/Vienna, Austria, April 2004

27. Yang, Z.: Multimodal aggression detection in trains, Ph.D. Dissertation, Delft University of Technology (2009), http://repository.tudelft.nl/view/ir/uuid%3A36f881a5-d443-48a1-982d-8f277fd23504/ (accessed April 2012)

28. Abdullah, L.N., Noah, S.: Integrating audio visual data for human action detection. In: Proceedings of the Fifth IEEE International Conference on Computer Graphics, Imaging and Visualisation CGIV 2008, pp. 242–246, Penang, Malaysia, August 2008

29. Zeng, Z., Tu, J., Pianfetti, B.M., Huang, T.S.: Audio–visual affective expression recognition through multistream fused HMM. IEEE Trans. Multimedia 10(4), 570–577 (2008)

30. Ros, J., Mekhnacha, K.: Multi-sensor human tracking with the Bayesian occupancy filter. In: Proceedings of the 16th International Conference on Digital Signal Processing DSP 2009, pp. 1–8, Santorini, Greece, July 2009

31. Stauffer, C., Grimson, W.E.L.: Adaptive background mixture models for real-time tracking. In: Proceedings of the IEEE Conference on Computer Vision and Pattern Recognition CVPR 1998, pp. 246–252, Ankorage, AK, USA, June 1998

32. Jain, R., Nagel, H.: On the analysis of accumulative difference pictures from image sequences of real world scenes. IEEE Trans. Pattern Anal. Mach. Intell. 1(2), 206–214 (1979)

33. Wren, C.R., Azarbayejani, A, Darrel, T., Pentland, A.P.: Pfinder: real-time tracking of the human body. IEEE Trans. Pattern Anal. Mach. Intell. 19(7), 780–785 (1997)

34. Stauffer, C., Grimson, W.E.L.: Learning patterns of activity using real-time tracking. IEEE Trans. Pattern Anal. Mach. Intell. 22(8), 747–767 (2000)

35. Elgammal, A., Harwood, D., Davis, L.: Non-parametric model for background subtraction. In: Proceedings of the European Conference on Computer Vision ECCV 2000, pp. 751–767, Dublin, Ireland, June–July 2000

36. Li, L., Leung, M.: Integrating intensity and texture differences for robust change detection. IEEE Trans. Image Process. 11(2), 105–112 (2002)

37. McKenna, S.J., Jabri, S., Duric, Z., Wechsler, H.: Tracking interacting people. In: Proceedings of the IEEE International Conference on Automatic Face and Gesture Recognition FG 2000, pp. 348–353, Grenoble, France, March 2000

38. Cucchiara, R., Grana, C., Piccardi, M., Prati A.: Detecting moving objects, ghosts, and shadows in video streams. IEEE Trans. Pattern Anal. Mach. Intell. 25(10), 1337–1342 (2003)

39. Meng, F., Guo, B., Fang, Y.: Novel image retrieval method based on interest points. In: Proceedings of the International Congress on Image and Signal Processing CISP 2010, pp. 1582–1585, Yantai, China, Oct 2010

40. Meng, F., Guo, B., Guo, L.: Image retrieval based on 2D histogram of interest points. In: Proceedings of the Fifth International Conference on Information Assurance and Security IAS 2009, pp. 250–253, Xi'An, China, August 2009

41. Serby, D., Meier, E.K., Van Gool, L.: Probabilistic object tracking using multiple features. In: Proceedings of the 17th International Conference on Pattern Recognition ICPR 2004, pp. 184–187, Cambridge, UK

42. Quddus, A., Gabbouj, M.: Wavelet-based corner detection technique using optimal scale. Pattern Recogn. Lett. 23(1/3), 215–220 (2002)

43. Yeh, C.-H.: Wavelet-based corner detection using eigenvectors of covariance matrices. Pattern Recogn. Lett. **24**(15), 2797–2806 (2003)
44. Harris, C., Stephens, M.: A combined corner and edge detector. In: Proceedings of the Fourth Alvey Vision Conference AVC88, pp. 147–151, Manchester, UK, Aug–Sept 1988
45. Khan, J.F., Adhami, R.R., Bhuiyan, S.M.A.: Interest points detection based on local frequency information of an image. In: Proceedings of the IEEE SoutheastCon 2008, pp. 569–574, Huntsville, AL, USA, April 2008
46. Yao, A., Wang, G., Lin, X., Wang, H.: Kernel based articulated object tracking with scale adaptation and model update. In: Proceedings of the IEEE International Conference on Acoustics, Speech and Signal Processing ICASSP 2008, pp. 945–948, Las Vegas, NE, USA, March–April 2008
47. Ali, Z., Hussain, S., Taj, I.A.: Kernel based robust object tracking using model updates and Gaussian pyramids. In: Proceedings of the IEEE Symposium on Emerging Technologies ICET 2005, pp. 144–150, Islamabad, Pakistan, Sept 2005
48. Chakraborty, D., Patra, D.: Real time object tracking based on segmentation and kernel based method. In: Proceedings of the Fifth International Conference on Industrial and Information Systems ICIIS 2010, pp. 426–429, Mangalore, India, July–Aug 2010
49. Collins, R.T.: Mean-shift blob tracking through scale space. In: Proceedings of the IEEE Conference on Computer Vision and Pattern Recognition CVPR 2003, pp. 234–240, Madison, WI, USA, June 2003
50. Lindeberg, T.: Feature detection with automatic scale selection. Int. J. Comput. Vis. **30**(2), 79–116 (s1998)
51. Comaniciu, D., Ramesh, V., Meer, P.: Real-time tracking of non-rigid objects using mean shift. In: Proceedings of the IEEE Conference on Computer Vision and Pattern Recognition CVPR 2000, pp. 142–149, Hilton Head, SC, USA, June 2000
52. Kass, M., Witkin, A., Terzopoulos, D.: Snakes: Active contour models. Int. J. Comput. Vis. **1**(4), 321–331 (1988)
53. Amini, A.A., Weymouth, T.E., Jain, R.C.: Using dynamic programming for solving variational problems in vision. IEEE Trans. Pattern Anal. Mach. Intell. **12**(9), 855–867 (1990)
54. Malladi, R., Sethian, J.A., Vemuri, B.C.: Shape modeling with front propagation: a level set approach. IEEE Trans. Pattern Anal. Mach. Intell. **17**(2), 158–175 (1995)
55. Dokladal, P., Enficiaud, R., Dejnozkova, E.: Contour-based object tracking with gradient-based contour attraction field. In: Proceedings of the IEEE International Conference on Acoustics, Speech, and Signal Processing ICASSP 2004, pp. 17–20, Montreal, Canada, May 2004
56. Staib, L.H., Duncan, J.S.: Boundary finding with parametrically deformable models. IEEE Trans. Pattern Anal. Mach. Intell. **14**(11), 90–104 (1992)
57. Boudoukh, G., Leichter, I., Rivlin, E.: Visual tracking of object silhouettes. In: Proceedings of the 16th IEEE International Conference on Image Processing ICIP 2009, pp. 3625–3628, Cairo, Egypt, Nov 2009
58. Li, G., Franco, J.-S., Pollefeys, M.: Multi-object shape estimation and tracking from silhouette cues. In: Proceedings of the IEEE Conference on Computer Vision and Pattern Recognition CVPR 2008, pp. 1–8, Anchorage, Alaska, USA, June 2008
59. Comaniciu, D., Ramesh, V., Meer, P.: Kernel-based object tracking. IEEE Trans. Pattern Anal. Mach. Intell. **25**(5), 564–577 (2003)
60. Adam, A., Rivlin, E., Shimshoni, I.: Robust fragments-based tracking using the integral histogram. In: Proceedings of the IEEE Conference on Computer Vision and Pattern Recognition CVPR 2006, vol. 1, pp. 798–805, New York, USA, June 2006
61. VIVID database. https://www.sdms.afrl.af.mil (2012). Accessed April 2012
62. Ramanan, D., Forsyth, D.A.: Finding and tracking people from the bottom up. In: Proceedings of the IEEE Conference on Computer Vision and Pattern Recognition CVPR 2003, pp. 467–474, Madison, WI, USA, June 2003

63. Yan, J., Pollefeys, M.: A factorization-based approach for articulated nonrigid shape, motion and kinematic chain recovery from video. IEEE Trans. Pattern Anal. Mach. Intell. **30**(5), pp. 865–877 (2008)
64. Shafique, K., Shah, M.: A non-iterative greedy algorithm for multi-frame point correspondence. In: Proceedings of the Ninth IEEE International Conference on Computer Vision ICCV 2003, pp. 110–115, Nice, France, Oct 2003
65. Shaohua, Z., Chellappa, R., Moghaddam, B.: Adaptive visual tracking and recognition using particle filters. In: Proceedings of the IEEE International Conference on Multimedia and Expo ICME 2003, pp. 349–352, Baltimore, MD, USA, July 2003
66. Schweitzer, H., Bell, J.W., Wu, F.: Very fast template matching. In: Proceedings of the European Conference on Computer Vision ECCV 2002, pp. 358–372, Copenhagen, Denmark, May 2002
67. Jepson, A.D., Fleet, D.J., El-Maraghi, T.F.: Robust online appearance models for visual tracking. IEEE Trans. Pattern Anal. Mach. Intell. **25**(10), 1296–1311 (2003)
68. Yilmaz, A., Li, X., Shah, M.: Contour based object tracking with occlusion handling in video acquired using mobile cameras. IEEE Trans. Pattern Anal. Mach. Intell. **26**(11), 1531–1536 (2004)
69. Freifeld, O., Weiss, A., Zuffi, S., Black M.J.: Contour people: a parameterized model of 2D articulated human shape. In: Proceedings of the IEEE Conference on Computer Vision and Pattern Recognition CVPR 2010, pp. 639–646, San Francisco, CA, USA, June 2010
70. Ramanan, D., Forsyth, D.A.: Finding and tracking people from the bottom up. In: Proceedings of the IEEE Conference on Computer Vision and Pattern Recognition CVPR 2003, pp. 467–474, Madison, WI, USA, June 2003
71. Balan, A.O., Sigal, L., Black, M.J., Davis, J.E, Haussecker, H.W.: Detailed human shape and pose from images. In: Proceedings of the IEEE Conference on Computer Vision and Pattern Recognition CVPR 2007, pp. 1–8, Minneapolis, MI, USA, June 2007
72. Yilmaz, A., Javed, O., Shah, M.: Object tracking: a survey. ACM Comput. Surv. **38**(4), article no. 13 (2006)
73. Stauffer, C., Grimson, W.E.L.: Learning patterns of activity using real-time tracking. IEEE Trans. Pattern Anal. Mach. Intell. **22**(8), 747–757 (2000)
74. Johnson, N., Hogg, D.C.: Learning the distribution of object trajectories for event recognition. In: Proceedings of the 6th British Machine Vision Conference BMVC'95, pp. 583–592, Birmingham, UK, Sept 1995
75. Pedrycz, W., Amato, A., Di Lecce, V., Piuri, V.: Fuzzy clustering with partial supervision in organization and classification of digital image. IEEE Trans. Fuzzy Syst. **16**(4), 1008–1026 (2008)
76. Amato, A., Di Lecce, V., Pedrycz, W.: A multidimensional scaling based GUI to evaluate partial supervision effects on prototypes spatial localization in fuzzy clustering. In: Proceedings of the 12th International Conference on Fuzzy Theory and Technology in the 10th Joint Conference on Information Science JCIS 2007, Salt Lake City, UT, USA, July 2007
77. Boiman, O., Irani, M.: Detecting irregularities in images and in video. In: Proceedings of the IEEE International Conference on Computer Vision ICCV 2005, pp. 462–469, Beijing, China, Oct 2005
78. Junejo, I.N., Javed, O., Shah, M.: Multi feature path modeling for video surveillance. In: Proceedings of the 17th International Conference on Pattern Recognition ICPR 2004, pp. 716–719, Cambridge, UK, Aug 2004
79. Vasvani, N., Roy Chowdhury, A., Chellappa, R.: Activity recognition using the dynamics of the configuration of interacting objects. In: Proceedings of the 2003 IEEE Conference on Computer Vision and Pattern Recognition CVPR 2003, pp. 633–640, Madison, WI, USA, June 2003
80. Dryden, I.L., Mardia, K.V.: Statistical shape analysis. Wiley, UK (1998)

81. Chowdhury, A.K.R., Chellappa, R.: A factorization approach for activity recognition. In: Proceedings of the IEEE Conference on Computer Vision and Pattern Recognition CVPR 2003, pp. 41–48, June 2003
82. Tomasi, C., Kanade, T.: Shape and motion from image streams under orthography: a factorization method. Int. J. Comput. Vis. **9**(2), 137–154 (1992)
83. Xiang, T., Gong, S.: Beyond tracking: modelling activity and understanding behaviour. Int. J. Comput. Vis. **67**(1), 21–51 (2006)
84. Schwarz, G.E.: Estimating the dimension of a model. Ann. Stat. **6**(2), 461–464 (1978)
85. Robertson, N., Reid, I.: Behavior understanding in video: a combined method. In: Proceedings of the IEEE International Conference on Computer Vision ICCV 2005, pp. 808–815, Beijing, China, Oct 2005
86. Efros, A.A., Berg, A.C., Mori, G., Malik, J.: Recognizing action at a distance. In: Proceedings of the IEEE International Conference on Computer Vision ICCV 2003, pp. 726–733, Nice, France, Oct 2003
87. Bobick, A., Davis, J.: The recognition of human movement using temporal templates. IEEE Trans. Pattern Anal. Mach. Intell. **23**(3), 257–267 (2001)
88. Hu, M.: Visual pattern recognition by moment invariants. IRE Trans. Inf. Theory, **8**(2), 179–187 (1962)
89. Bradski, G.R., Davis, J.W.: Motion segmentation and pose recognition with motion history gradients. Mach. Vis. Appl. **13**(3), 174–184 (2002)
90. Yilmaz, A., Shah, M.: Actions sketch: a novel action representation. In: Proceedings of the IEEE Conference on Computer Vision and Pattern Recognition CVPR 2005, pp. 984–989, San Diego, CA, USA, June 2005
91. Yu, H., Sun, G.-M., Song, W.-X., Li, X.: Human motion recognition based on neural networks. In: Proceedings of the International Conference on Communications, Circuits and Systems ICCCAS 2005, pp. 979–982, Hong Kong, China, May 2005
92. Luo, Y., Wu, T.-W., Hwang, J.-N.: Object-based analysis and interpretation of human motion in sports video sequences by dynamic Bayesian networks. Comput. Vis. Image Underst. **92**(2/3), 196–216 (2003)
93. Shi, Y., Bobick, A., Essa, I.: Learning temporal sequence model from partially labeled data. In: Proceedings of the IEEE Conference on Computer Vision and Pattern Recognition CVPR 2006, pp. 1631–1638, New York, USA, June 2006
94. Davis, J.W., Taylor, S.R.: Analysis and recognition of walking movements. In: Proceedings of the International Conference on Pattern Recognition ICPR 2002, pp. 315–318, Quebec City, Canada, Aug 2002
95. Parameswaran, V., Chellappa, R.: View invariance for human action recognition. Int. J. Comput. Vis. **66**(1), 83–101 (2006)
96. Weiss, I., Ray, M.: Model-based recognition of 3D objects from single images. IEEE Trans. Pattern Anal. Mach. Intell. **23**(2), 116–128 (2001)
97. Gritai, A., Sheikh, Y., Shah, M.: On the use of anthropometry in the invariant analysis of human actions. In: Proceedings of the International Conference on Pattern Recognition ICPR 2004, pp. 923–926, Cambridge, UK, Aug 2004
98. Bailey, R.W.: Human performance engineering: a guide for system designers. Prentice-Hall, NJ (1982)
99. Ivanov, Y., Bobick, A: Recognition of visual activities and interactions by stochastic parsing. IEEE Trans. Pattern Anal. Mach. Intell. **22**(8), 852–872 (2000)
100. Rao, C., Yilmaz, A., Shah, M.: View-invariant representation and recognition of actions. Int. J. Comput. Vis. **50**(2), 203–226 (2002)
101. Del Vecchio, D., Murray, R.M., Perona, P.: Decomposition of human motion into dynamics-based primitives with application to drawing tasks. Automatica **39**(12), 2085–2098 (2003)
102. Lu, C., Ferrier, N.: Repetitive motion analysis: segmentation and event classification. IEEE Trans. Pattern Anal. Mach. Intell. **26**(2), 258–263 (2004)

103. Jagacinski, R.J., Johnson, W.W., Miller, R.A: Quantifying the cognitive trajectories of extrapolated movements. J. Exp. Psychol.: Hum. Percept. Perform. **9**(1), 43–57 (1983)
104. Rubin, J.M., Richards, W.A: Boundaries of visual motion. Technical Report AIM-835, Massachusetts Institute of Technology, Artificial Intelligence Laboratory, April 1985
105. Zacks, J., Tversky, B.: Event structure in perception and cognition. Psychol. Bull. **127**(1), 3–21 (2001)
106. Park, S., Aggarwal, J.K.: Semantic-level understanding of human actions and interactions using event hierarchy. In: Proceedings of the Workshop on Articulated and Non-Rigid Motion in the IEEE Conference on Computer Vision and Pattern Recognition CVPR 2004, p. 12, Washington, DC, USA, June 2004
107. Francke, H., Del Solar, J.R., Verschae, R.: Real-time hand gesture detection and recognition using boosted classifiers and active learning. In: Advances in Image and Video Technology, pp. 533–547, Springer, New York (2007)
108. Holte, M., Moeslund T.: View invariant gesture recognition using 3D motion primitives. In: Proceedings of the IEEE International Conference on Acoustics, Speech and Signal Processing ICASSP 2008, pp. 797–800, Las Vegas, NE, USA, Mar–April 2008
109. Lee S.-W.: Automatic gesture recognition for intelligent human-robot interaction. In: Proceedings of the IEEE International Conference on Automatic Face and Gesture Recognition FGR 2006, pp. 645–650, Southampton, UK, April 2006
110. Park, H.S., Jung D.J., Kim H.J.: Vision-based game interface using human gesture. In: Advances in Image and Video Technology, pp. 662–671, Springer, New York (2006)
111. Ye, G., Corso, J.J., Burschka, D., Hager, G.D.: VICs: a modular HCI framework using spatiotemporal dynamics. Mach. Vis. Appl. **16**(1), 13–20 (2004)
112. Yilmaz, A.: Recognizing human actions in videos acquired by uncalibrated moving cameras. In: Proceedings of the IEEE International Conference on Computer Vision ICCV 2005, pp. 150–157, Beijing, China, Oct 2005
113. Weinland, D., Ronfard, R., Boyer E.: Free viewpoint action recognition using motion history volumes. Comp. Vis. Image Underst. **104**(2/3), 249–257 (2006)
114. Gorelick, L., Blank, M., Shechtman, E., Irani, M., Basri, R.: Actions as space-time shapes. In: Proceedings of the IEEE International Conference on Computer Vision ICCV 2005, pp. 1395–1402, Beijing, China, Oct 2005
115. Lv, F., Nevatia, R.: Single view human action recognition using key pose matching and Viterbi path searching. In: Proceedings of the IEEE Conference on Computer Vision and Pattern Recognition CVPR 2007, pp. 1–8, Minneapolis, MI, USA, June 2007
116. Peng, B., Qian, G., Rajko, S.: View-invariant full-body gesture recognition from video. In: Proceedings of the 19th International Conference on Pattern Recognition ICPR 2008, pp. 1–5, Tampa, FL, USA, Dec 2008
117. Amato, A.: A SOM and feature based solution for correspondence problem in binocular vision. In: Proceedings of the IEEE International Conference on Computational Intelligence for Measurement Systems and Applications CIMSA 2010, pp. 38–42, Taranto, Italy, Sept 2010
118. Amato, A., Piuri, V., Di Lecce, V.: An image retrieval based solution for correspondence problem in binocular vision. In: Proceedings of the IEEE-RIVF International Conference on Computing and Communication Technologies RIVF 2010, pp. 1–6, Hanoi, Vietnam, Nov 2010
119. Zitnick C. L., Kanade, T.: A cooperative algorithm for stereo matching and occlusion detection. IEEE Trans. Pattern Anal. Mach. Intell. **22**(7), 675–684 (2000)
120. Yoon, S., Park, S.K., Kang, S., Kwak, Y.K.: Fast correlation-based stereomatching with the reduction of systematic errors. Pattern Recogn. Lett. **26**(14), 2221–2231 (2005)
121. Venkatesh, Y.V., Kumar, R.S., Kumar, J.A.: On the application of a modified self-organizing neural network to estimate stereo disparity. IEEE Trans. Image Process. **16**(11), 2822–2829 (2007)
122. Yang, L., Wang, R., Ge, P., Cao, F.: Research on area-matching algorithm based on feature-matching constraints. In: Proceedings of the Fifth International Conference on Natural Computation ICNC 2009, pp. 208–213, Tianjian, China, Aug 2009

123. Sun, J., Zheng, N., Shum, H.: Stereo matching using belief propagation. IEEE Trans. Pattern Anal. Mach. Intell. 25(7), 787–800 (2003)
124. Ruichek, Y.: A hierarchical neural stereo matching approach for real-time obstacle detection using linear cameras. In: Proceedings of the IEEE Intelligent Transportation Systems Conference ITSC 2003, pp. 299–304, Stuttgart, Germany, Oct 2003
125. Krumm, J., Harris, S., Meyers, B., Brumitt, B., Hale, M., Shafer, S.: Multi-camera multi-person tracking for easy living. In: Proceedings of the IEEE International Workshop on Visual Surveillance, pp. 3–10, Dublin, Ireland, July 2000
126. Mittal, A., Davis, L.: M2tracker: a multi-view approach to segmenting and tracking people in a cluttered scene using region-based stereo. In: Proceedings of the 7th European Conference on Computer Vision, pp. 18–36, Copenhagen, Denmark, May 2002
127. Hu, W., Hu, M., Zhou, X., Tan, T., Lou, J., Maybank, S.: Principal axis based correspondence between multiple cameras for people tracking. IEEE Trans. Pattern Anal. Mach. Intell. 28(4), 663–671 (2006)
128. Khan, S., Shah, M.: Consistent labeling of tracked objects in multiple cameras with overlapping fields of view. IEEE Trans. Pattern Anal. Mach. Intell. 25(10), 1355–1360 (2003)
129. Xu, G., Zhang, Z.: Epipolar geometry in stereo, motion and object recognition: a unified approach. Kluwer Academic Publishers, Dordrecht (2010)
130. Wren, C., Azarbayejani, A., Darrell, T., Pentland, A.P.: Pfinder: real-time tracking of the human body. IEEE Trans. Pattern Anal. Mach. Intell. 19(7), 780–785 (1997)
131. Cucchiara, R., Piccardi, M., Prati, A.: Detecting moving objects, ghosts, and shadows in video streams. IEEE Trans. Pattern Anal. Mach. Intell. 25(10), 1337–1342 (2003)
132. Di Lecce, V., Amato, A.: A fuzzy logic based approach to feedback reinforcement in image retrieval. In: Proceedings of the International Conference on Intelligent Computing ICIC'09, pp. 939–947, Ulsan, South Korea, Sept 2009
133. Amato, A., Di Lecce, V., Piuri, V.: An image retrieval interface based on dynamic knowledge. In: Proceedings of 2005 International Conference on Computational Intelligence for Modelling, Control and Automation, and 2005 International Conference on Intelligent Agents, Web Technologies and Internet Commerce CIMCA-IAWTIC'05, pp. 641–646, Vienna, Austria, Nov 2005
134. Amato, A., Di Lecce, V., Piuri, V.: An interface for semantic browsing of an images database. In: Proceedings of the IEEE International Conference on Virtual Environments, Human-Computer Interfaces and Measurement Systems VECIMS 2004, pp. 67–71, Boston, MA, USA, June 2004
135. Santini, S., Jain, R.: The 'El Niño' image database system. Procedings of the IEEE International Conference on Multimedia Computing and Systems ICMCS'99, pp. 524–529, Florence, Italy, June 1999
136. Tversky, A.: Features of similarity. Psychol. Rev. 84(4), 327–352 (1977)
137. Amato, A., Delvecchio, T., Di Lecce, V.: Silhouettes based evaluation of the effectiveness in image retrieval. In: Proceedings of the 6th CSCC Multiconference, pp. 169–176, Rethymno, Crete Island, Greece, July 2002
138. Kruskal, J.B.: Multi-dimensional scaling by optimizing goodness-of-fit to a non-metric hypobook. Psychometrika 29(1), 1–27 (1964)
139. Amato, A., Di Lecce, V.: A knowledge based approach for a fast image retrieval system. Image and Vision Computing, vol. 26(11, November 2008, pp. 1466-1480
140. Iqbal, Q., Aggarwal, K.: Feature integration, multi-image queries and relevance feedback in image retrieval. In: Proceedings of the 6th International Conference on Visual Information Systems VISUAL 2003, pp. 467–474, Miami, FL, USA, Sept 2003
141. Amato, A., Di Lecce, V., Piuri, V.: A new graphical interface for web search engine. In: Proceedings of the IEEE Conference on Virtual Environments, Human-Computer Interfaces and Measurement Systems VECIMS'07, pp. 42–46, Ostuni, Italy, June 2007
142. Smith, A.R.: Color gamut transform pairs. ACM SIGGRAPH Comput. Graph. 12(3), 12–19 (1978)

143. Ojala, T., Rautiainen, M., Matinmikko, E., Aittola, M.: Semantic image retrieval with HSV correlograms. In: Proceedings of the 12th Scandinavian Conference on Image Analysis SCIA 2001, pp. 621–627, Bergen, Norway, June 2001

144. Smith, J.R.: Integrated spatial feature image systems: retrieval, analysis and compression. Ph.D. Dissertation, Graduate School of Arts and Sciences, Columbia University (1997)

145. Grgic, M., Ghanbari, M., Grgic, S.: Texture-based image retrieval in MPEG-7 multimedia system. In: Proceedings of the International Conference on Trends in Communications EUROCON'01, pp. 365–368, Bratislava, Slovakia, July 2001

146. Zhang, J., Tan, T.: Brief review of invariant texture analysis methods. Pattern Recogn. 35(3), 735–747 (2002)

147. Grigorescu, S.E., Petkov, N., Kruizinga, P.: A comparative study of filter based texture operators using Mahalanobis distance. In: Proceedings of the 15th International Conference on Pattern Recognition ICPR 2000, pp. 885–888, Barcelona, Spain, Sept 2000

148. Stottinger, J., Hanbury, A., Gevers, T., Sebe, N.: Lonely but attractive: sparse color salient points for object retrieval and categorization. In: Proceedings of the IEEE Conference on Computer Vision and Pattern Recognition CVPR2009, pp. 1–8, Miami, Florida, USA, June 2009

149. Jian, M., Ma, P., Chen, S.: Content-based image retrieval using salient points and spatial distribution. In: Proceedings of the International Symposium on Information Science and Engineering ISISE 2008, pp. 687–690, Shanghai, China, Dec 2008

150. Patras, I., Andreopoulos, Y.: Incremental salient point detection. In: Proceedings of the IEEE International Conference on Acoustics, Speech and Signal Processing ICASSP 2008, pp. 1337–1340, Las Vegas, NE, USA, Mar–April 2008

151. Sebe, N., Tian, Q., Loupias, E., Lew, M.S., Huang, T.S.: Evaluation of salient point techniques. Image Vis. Comput. 21(13–14), 1087–1095 (2003)

152. Martin, J.C.: Introduction to languages and the theory of computation, McGraw-Hill, New York (2011)

153. Ester, M., Kriegel. H.P., Sander, J., Xu, X.: A density-based algorithm for discovering clusters in large spatial databases with noise. In: Proceedings of the Second International Conference on Knowledge Discovery and Data Mining KDD'96, pp. 226–231, Portland, OR, USA, Aug 2006

154. Pauwels, E.J., Fiddelaers, P., Van Gool, L.: DOG-based unsupervized clustering for CBIR. In: Proceedings of the Second International Conference on Visual Information Systems VISUAL 1997, pp. 13–20, San Diego, CA, USA, Dec 1997

155. Amato, A., Di Lecce, V., Piuri, V.: Neural network based video surveillance system. In: Proceedings of the IEEE International Conference on Computational Intelligence for Homeland Security and Personal Safety CIHSPS 2005, pp. 85–89, Orlando, FL, USA, Mar–April 2005

156. Amato, A., Di Lecce, V., Piuri, V.: Knowledge based video surveillance system. In: Proceedings of the 14th International Conference on Computer Theory and Application ICCTA 2004, Alexandria, Egypt, Sept 2004

157. Majecka, B.: Statistical models of pedestrian behavior in the forum. M.Sc. Dissertation, School of Informatics, University of Edinburgh (2009)

158. Edinburgh Informatics Forum Pedestrian Database, http://homepages.inf.ed.ac.uk/rbf/FORUMTRACKING/. Accessed May 2012

159. August 24 Tracks, Edinburgh Informatics Forum Pedestrian Database, http://homepages.inf.ed.ac.uk/rbf/FORUMTRACKING/SINGH/tracks.Aug24.zip. Accessed May 2012